UNTIL THERE ARE

UNTIL THERE ARE

N0NE

BIBLE TRANSLATION, LIFE TRANSFORMATION,
AND SEED COMPANY'S FIRST 25 YEARS

Seed Company™
Bible Translation. Life Transformation.

Printed in the United States of America

ISBN: 978-0-692-98301-0
LCCN: 2017960497

First Edition

In honor of all Seed Company global staff who have served over the past 25 years. They are the unsung heroes and will be welcomed with joy into Heaven by those who have gained access to Scripture.

"His master replied, 'Well done, good and faithful servant! You have been faithful with a few things; I will put you in charge of many things. Come and share your master's happiness!'"

—Matthew 25:21 (NIV)

Going back to where Seed Company's journey begins, so much has changed. There is much to praise God for when we look at 25 years of God-sized vision and provision! This collection of milestone stories gives us a glimpse into inspiring progress, fueled by persevering prayer and partnership with faithful stewards.

Yet, nothing has changed. The vision to serve and empower national visionaries is where it all began. The way this is done may have evolved, and has certainly grown in both innovation and impact. But the main thing is still very much the main thing. In my experience, the generosity of Seed Company and its people extends far beyond the sharing of strategic support to build others up. Every exchange brings with it a refreshing tone of encouragement—an infusion of faith and joyful service—making partnership with Seed Company a most memorable journey of kingdom friendship.

I heartily endorse this unfolding story and its call to press on to the day when there are finally none!

Karen Floor
Chief Executive Officer
Wycliffe South Africa

Partnering with Seed Company means investing in others' eternal destinies. My wife, Cara, and I feel the urgency of reaching Bibleless people worldwide. The stories in this book demonstrate the tremendous impact of Bible translation both for today and for eternity.

Lance Berkman
Former Major League Baseball Player
Recognized by Forbes (2012) as one of the "30 Most Generous Celebrities"

Samuel Chiang's account of the progress of Bible translation through Seed Company is absolutely riveting. Their servant spirit and unending creativity have allowed them to provide the leadership and expertise in Scripture translation in the most remote areas of the Earth. I count it one of the great joys of my life to work in partnership with Seed Company throughout the world.

Paul Eshleman
Vice President
Campus Crusade for Christ International (Cru)

CONTENTS

PART III
Restoring Each Community

PART IV
Rediscovering the Global Body of Christ

PART V
Rallying All: The Acceleration of Bible Translation

FOREWORD

For a number of years I had the honor of serving on the Wycliffe USA Board of Directors while Bernie May was our President. During those years, Bernie and I developed a deep and lasting friendship, which was to mature and develop in wonderful new directions with the advent of Seed Company. In 1992, our Wycliffe Board fashioned a new path of service for Bernie as he was stepping down as President. We unanimously decided to make him the Vice President of New Ventures and to turn him loose to try new things and see where God would lead.

Bernie had thought and prayed about new ideas for Bible translation and wondered whether it might be possible to use national mother tongue translators to do the translation work, and also to raise money from individual donors for each language. The first 10 people he asked all said, "Yes, I would love to support my own language translation!"

With those commitments in hand, Bernie settled into a small office in the corner of the headquarters building in Huntington Beach, California, in 1993 and gathered a few people to work with him on this new program. This marked the informal beginning of Seed Company.

By the end of 1996, Bernie's efforts were bearing fruit. Enough growth was happening that he knew the next question was how to structure this effort for long-term success. He asked me if I would lead a task force to work this through and make a recommendation to the Wycliffe Board. The task force met, and we quickly focused on the need for a structure that would allow maximum creativity and innovation, not constrained by cultural and historic ways of doing things. We dreamed that this new group might provide a source of ideas, input, and alternate ways of doing things that would be useful to the entire world of Bible translation.

These key conclusions led us to recommend a new, separate corporation with its own board, but still within the broad world of Wycliffe. When this was presented to Wycliffe in 1998 they were unanimous in affirmation and approval, and I was asked to become the first Chairman.

Now the task shifted to developing a board, and a rapidly growing team committed to these new approaches. But how could the board be different if we wanted to be such a young, innovative, and different organization?

We decided to create a younger board with an average age of all members at any time of 50 or less. This was an exciting idea that over the years has paid off enormously in a vibrant, committed, and highly valuable board. By 1999, we realized as it grew that the organization needed core values to ground and direct our thinking. So we got the team together for two days of studying God's Word, prayer, discussion, laughter, food, and talking about what was really important. At the end, we came out completely committed to five core values that have guided the work ever since: (1) honoring God in all we do; (2) valuing individuals and relationships; (3) partnering effectively; (4) encouraging creativity and innovation; and (5) managing for quality results.

As is true in many successful, long-term organizations, these early years were full of excitement, growth, and opportunity. They were also full of the challenge of wondering whether this whole thing would work, and of never quite knowing what the next step might be.

At every step along the way, we asked God to show us where He wanted us to go, and how to move forward. Not everything we tried worked, but most of it did. Bernie's initial assumptions about the attraction of the model to donors and the availability of quality mother tongue translators proved correct.

Today, we stand at the threshold of a world in which everyone might have access to God's Word in their heart language whether they are traditional cultures, the Deaf, oral learners, small people groups or larger ones, in closed countries or open.

Lord, we ask You to continue to guide us as You have so faithfully. We ask You to help us to stay humble and responsive to your direction. And together with You we hope for a world in which every person can hear the name of Christ in a language they understand. Amen.

Peter Ochs
Founding Seed Company Board Chairman

PREFACE
THE PRIORITY OF PRAYER

Back in the early 1980s, when I had just been appointed President of Wycliffe Bible Translators, I attended a strategic planning seminar for young executives. The instructor began with a rather obvious question: "What is the goal of your organization?"

That was easy. Wycliffe's mission was (and still is today) to translate the Bible into every language of the world. Although simple to summarize, the mission itself was giant. At the rate of Bible translation in 1981, it was projected that finishing the job would take about 200 years.

Then, the instructor posed a second question, a harder one: "What is the single, most important thing you can do as Chief Executive Officer to advance your organization toward that goal?"

I am embarrassed at how long it took me to come up with the right answer. I thought first of resources—people and funds. If we had greater numbers of people and more funding, then we could make a lot of headway. Somehow, that response didn't seem right. Then, the Holy Spirit helped me see the true answer: prayer.

As I thought more about prayer, I realized we were focusing our spiritual petitions on where missionaries were present, instead of on the places and people without them. What if we began praying for the people groups and languages of the world that had no missionaries and no Bibles?

In *Ethnologue*, a publication listing the world's known languages and the availability of Scripture in each, I saw there were about 3,000 unreached language groups. That night, my wife and I prayerfully searched *Ethnologue* and chose the Dubu, a small people group in Indonesia, to pray for. They were so isolated that no one knew much about them, except that an anthropologist had traveled in this region and discovered a village of 220 people speaking this unknown language.

So in 1981, we began praying daily for the Dubu. Soon after, I extended the invitation for others to join us in prayer. I wrote an article for Wycliffe's flagship magazine that was sent to constituents and partners. In it, I challenged readers to make a similar commitment to pray daily, by name, for one of the world's Bibleless people groups. I offered to send a name to each person who expressed interest.

The response was so incredible that we organized a program and launched Wycliffe's Bibleless Peoples Prayer Project. We focused this great resource—the prayers of many—on the strategic need to see God's Word made available in all of these unreached languages. I was overjoyed to witness God's people's commitment to pray for the lost.

But, after eight years of praying daily for the Dubu, I hit a wall. I began to feel discouraged. I had been praying that someone would take the Gospel to them, but it wasn't happening. Then, I believe God prompted me with a new thought: pray specifically that one or more of the Dubu would travel outside their isolated village to an Indonesian city where they could hear the Gospel. It seemed to make sense, and thankfully it was something new to pray for. In faith, I prayed on.

A year later, I heard from a missionary in the area that what I had prayed for had happened. One of the Dubu men had traveled to Sentani, a large coastal town, to seek work. It happened that he sought housing with a Christian family who told him about Jesus. There, he accepted Christ and a year later he returned to the village and called a meeting of the whole tribe, who also accepted Jesus as Savior.

In recent years, I have learned the Dubu church is doing well. They report sending out four evangelists to other Dubu villages to share the Gospel. The latest news is that two young men with a desire to translate the Bible into their own language are in a Bible school in the city.

God is doing exceedingly more than we could ask or think for the Dubu people.

Thirty years after our first prayer for them, my faith is unwavering. God wants them to have His Word in the language they understand best—Dubu.

But I continue to pray for the Dubu. It is perhaps the single most important thing I can do to help advance this goal.

> *The LORD did not set his affection on you and choose you because you were more numerous than other peoples, for you were the fewest of all peoples. But it was because the LORD loved you and kept the oath he swore to your ancestors that he brought you out with a mighty hand and redeemed you from the land of slavery, from the power of Pharaoh king of Egypt.*
>
> *—Deuteronomy 7:7–8 (NIV)*

Bernie May
Seed Company Founder

INTRODUCTION

In 1993, I was serving in Hong Kong with Partners International. During a week of staff meetings in the U.S., our Chief Executive Officer, Chuck Bennett, came into the office. He gathered us to announce that a friend of his had an intriguing plan.

The friend was Bernie May. The plan, birthed during a season of intense prayer, was to accelerate Bible translation, starting with 10 projects and 10 major financial partners. Bernie foresaw that God's resources would increasingly be both in the West and in the Majority World. The Western focus could shift to helping indigenous leaders translate Scripture in their own languages.

The entity to drive this idea would become known as Seed Company. Little did I know then that one day I would play a role in the future that Bernie envisioned and that today's Bible translation movement would be looking at the very real possibility of heart language Scripture reaching all people in our generation.

I still recall the day in 2011, in Hawaii, when Roy Peterson, current President and CEO of American Bible Society and then President and CEO at Seed Company, spoke with me about becoming a Seed Company Board member. He indicated the length of service was to be nine years.

I had a lump in my throat (this was a lengthy commitment), and I told him that I must pray about it. My bride, Robbi, and I have always committed to serving just one board at a time. After prayerful consideration, I was interviewed by Todd Peterson, Chairman of the board, along with Bill Williams, board member and the CEO of National Christian Foundation. Eventually, I was invited to serve on the board.

There are *four unique qualities* that Seed Company possesses which I have observed while serving on the Seed Company Board and now as President and CEO. Some may call this the governance board's DNA.

First and foremost, this is a *board-led organization*. The leadership of the board drives the vision and outcomes. Peter Ochs, the founding board chair, not only fostered the business principles and disciplines for the organization, but also encouraged risk-taking and innovations for the sake of acceleration in Bible translation.

The camaraderie of the board is deeply *rooted in relationships*, and the average age of the entire board should be less than 50. Undergirding the practices of risk-taking and innovation is the continual recruitment of younger board members who are able to see things differently and contribute thoughts uniquely. The integration of new and veteran board members can only really work when there is an even deeper set of values at work. This intangible—some call it chemistry—is what the Seed Company Board simply calls "rooted in relationships."

Generosity is a word that is modeled by the board. What does one do with board members who have served for nine years and have not yet reached 40 years of age? Usually, most boards would rotate them off for one year, and then bring them back on again. Not at Seed Company. They are not recruited back onto the board; instead, they are released to the kingdom to serve on other boards because we believe that their experiences from serving on the Seed Company Board are to be shared.

I still recall the day in the September 2014 board meeting when Todd Peterson, then Interim President and CEO, spoke about illumiNations (our fundraising gathering) and proposed that it be given to the entire Bible translation movement. We all agreed it was a good idea to do this so that more funding could be raised to eradicate Bible poverty. This is generosity at work.

Finally, there is a *fervency*, *urgency*, and *prayerful consideration* of reaching all the Bibleless peoples of the world. The measurement and accountability process is such that the focus is on both access and impact of First Scriptures for those who are Bibleless. From the ground up before every translation project, 10 people are recruited and commit to pray regularly for the lifetime of the project.

The board gives strong leadership by praying regularly for major events, including illumiNations and forWORD. These annual gatherings play a pivotal part in our goal of growing partnerships with kingdom investors. We have a regular cadence of calls prior to each event where we include spouses. I am always moved by their deep intercession with God for the Bibleless peoples of the world.

From Peter Ochs to Judy Sweeney to Todd Peterson to Rick Britton to Joyce Williams, each Seed Company Board Chair has brought relentless focus on outcomes and results. Rooted in relationships, the board has modeled generosity, prayer, and an expectant belief in God that all remaining languages will receive some Scripture in their heart language by 2025.

My own journey into the current role also included serving on the board search committee to find the next CEO. Even with solid candidates available, I was requested to step off the search committee in order to become a candidate. Quite frankly, I was thoroughly enjoying what I was doing. But God met me in a unique way in West Africa during the Ebola crisis. Out of obedience to God, I submitted my name as a candidate and successfully went through the interview process.

Moving from a governance role into an operational role, I am even more thrilled with my deeper connections to today's list of Bible translation heroes, which includes more people from more countries than ever before. As the Global Church grows and matures, the Great Commission's local task of making disciples falls to local churches everywhere. Bible translation in its many forms—oral, print, audio files, and sign language—transforms lives wherever it goes. It is truly an amazing time to be part of this movement of God!

As we discussed how to reflect Seed Company's 25-year history in book form, one thing became clear: While there's certainly a place for institutional history books (timelines and mission statements, boards and buildings), we wanted most to tell Seed Company's story through the eyes of those whose lives are being changed as they encounter God's Word. It is a window not only into Seed Company, but also into how God worked in and through people.

You hold in your hands a compilation of 25 impact stories from around the globe. All highlight strategies that accelerate Bible translation. Some contain pseudonyms because they're happening right now in places where spiritual and political opposition run high. This work grows increasingly dangerous.

Sprinkled throughout the chapters are the names of a few of our global colleagues: the life, veins, and connections to both language communities and investors. They represent a community of dedicated Bible translators across the world. For our field colleagues who are connected to the local translation partners, most of what they do is unseen.

For example, when we talk about an active project, most will not realize that our field colleagues might have had that same project in the pipeline for three to four years so that it is ready for accelerated Bible translation. They are the quiet ones who hold up the arms of the local "Moses" as pictured in Exodus 17:12. It is humbling to serve alongside each of these men and women.

As you move through the chapters and stories, you will also find the reflections of 25 individuals or couples—financial, prayer, and organizational partners who have participated with God in the journey of Bible translation. They, and thousands like them, play hugely significant roles in this amazing story that God continues to write. What an honor and privilege we all feel every day to be part of it all. Glory to God!

Samuel E. Chiang
President and Chief Executive Officer, Seed Company

February 2018

Near Eastern Sun, by Hyatt Moore

PART I

GRAND VISIONS OF NEW BEGINNINGS

CHAPTER 1

SEED COMPANY BEGINNINGS

Through intense prayer and unconventional thinking, a bold idea with few initial takers became the future of Bible translation.

Bernie May believed God wanted to do something different within the Bible translation movement. But the man who would become the first President of Seed Company wasn't convinced he should be part of it.

The year was 1992, and Bernie had worked with Wycliffe Bible Translators (WBT) since 1954. His 12 years as Wycliffe USA's leader had just ended. At 60, he needed a break. But change was coming in Bible translation, and the Wycliffe USA Board, led by Chairman Peter Ochs, asked Bernie to spearhead the transformation.

"I'll pray about it," Bernie told him.

Bernie knew that change was needed.

Back in 1975, with nationalism on the rise globally, Wycliffe had established national Bible translation organizations around the world with a "three-self" concept: self-determining, self-propagating, and self-funding.

Bernie May helped launch what would become Seed Company in 1993 under Wycliffe Bible Translators, with the name Partners With Nationals. The initiative's key concept of coupling investors directly with national-run translation projects rose from months of intense prayer and consultation with charter investors.

Photo: Seed Company

"They were real good at self-determining—they liked being in charge," Bernie recalled. "They were OK with self-propagating to get more people. But the self-funding part didn't work very well, and they kept depending on outside sources for funding."

With a support system dependent upon raising money for, essentially, outsiders working in a nationalist climate, funding remained an issue into the 1980s.

"By the end of the decade," Bernie said, "it just wasn't working."

As the 1990s began, John Bendor-Samuel was nearing the conclusion of his term leading the Summer Institute of Linguistics (SIL) and surveyed Bible translation's long-term needs. He saw that Africa was different from other locations, already strong in linguistics and with advanced capabilities for Bible translation.

Accelerating Bible translation in Africa and, subsequently, other regions would require a new strategy. In 1991, John pitched his final challenge to the joint board of directors for Wycliffe and SIL: find a way to fund the national organizations.

Those boards soon turned to Wycliffe USA to develop a program to provide that funding. The Wycliffe USA Board knew that Bernie could find a way.

"A brilliant visionary," Hyatt Moore, Bernie's replacement as Wycliffe USA President, called him.

"Bernie May," said David Bendor-Samuel, SIL Vice President at the time and John's brother, "was very open to opportunities which didn't really look like opportunities." Bernie took an eight-month sabbatical to pray and travel the United States with his wife, meeting with donors he had developed relationships with through WBT.

They were mature Christians, he said, who understood missions.

He intentionally sought the input of what he called "outsiders"—successful business leaders working outside of Bible translation yet also involved in and knowledgeable of the movement. Bernie leaned heavily on Ochs and Roger Tompkins, who, like Ochs, was a businessman who had chaired the Wycliffe USA Board. A strategy began to develop, and each person Bernie visited encouraged him to move forward with his vision.

I'll do it, Bernie decided.

With Hyatt's full support, a new organization spun out of Wycliffe USA for the purpose of accelerating Bible translation.

On January 1, 1993, an experiment began that would become known as Seed Company. Bernie led the way from his desk inside a converted broom closet at Wycliffe USA headquarters in California. And it launched on a model drastically different for the Bible translation movement: funding projects rather than missionaries through individuals capable of investing, in some cases, 100 times the typical contributions that supported Wycliffe's work.

Investing was a key word. During his sabbatical, Bernie had noticed Wycliffe's donor base changing its collective mindset. Donating was giving way to investing, and Bernie's strategy included an outcome-based framework with increased accountability. Project management became a priority.

"An investor expects to be part of the process and see results," he said.

The new model centered on partnering with national Bible translation organizations. Locals would help lead—and would own—projects to translate Scripture into their heart languages.

"I had a sense that's what God wanted us to try," Bernie said. "I could sense God in it."

Not everyone could.

"There were a lot of people who didn't think Seed Company was even needed."

Bernie met with SIL's area directors for Africa, Asia, and the Americas. Only the director of Africa—the area that was a pioneer in the need for nationals-led translation—embraced his proposal.

The area director for Asia, who was a close friend, told Bernie he appreciated the approach but didn't think it would be embraced there.

Bernie returned home asking himself, *Why am I doing this?*

After all, he had designed the model specifically to better assist field partners. He had anticipated broad support for this new type of partnership. Yet the Americas and now Asia—Bible translation's largest field of the future—had turned him down.

Maybe I'm doing the wrong thing, he thought. *Maybe it's not going to work.* But he set to work anyway.

Bernie targeted 10 projects where he believed the strategy would succeed. Then, he began approaching businessmen he hoped would invest $10,000 a year for up to 10 years. He only had to contact 10 potential investors, because all said yes.

Soon after that, Bernie shared his vision with Ken Taylor, Founder of Tyndale House Publishers and creator of The Living Bible.

"I want to encourage you," Ken told Bernie. "I'm going to give you $100,000 each year for the next five years."

"I'm encouraged already," Bernie said.

The experiment worked, and in 1998, Seed Company incorporated. Ochs was the first Chairman of the board.

"He was a very, very key player," Bernie said. "He had a lot of good ideas. A lot of what Seed Company is doing now and the early policies that made us distinctive came from Peter. He made us function like a business, and none of us knew how to do that."

And now, 25 years after its start in a broom closet, Seed Company not only operates in the places that initially said "no, thanks" to Bernie, but also in locations once thought too risky, and even impossible, for Bible translators to work. The Seed Company model is employed throughout the movement as Common Framework. As a result, a movement once focused on the *next* group of languages needing Scripture is targeting the *final* languages.

Bernie reflected on Seed Company's history by recalling his junior high days, when he ran track relays. The anticipation swelled with each baton handoff. The cheering increased as the finish line neared.

Spreading the Gospel has been like a relay race, he continued. The Apostle Paul ran the first leg 2,000 years ago. Now, Bernie said, the race is in the final lap, and he relishes being part of the excitement.

"Here's something that's taken generations," he said, "and we might be the generation that carries it over the line."

Joyce Williams

Joyce Williams is Chairwoman of the Seed Company Board. She and her husband, Ron, first became acquainted with Seed Company as donors. Joyce has more than 25 years of cumulative board governance experience in faith-based organizations.

The beginning of the Great Commission is God's Word. How can people be saved, how can they know Christ, how can their lives and communities be changed without knowing Christ? We know Christ through his Word. And to know Him through your heart language, to be able to really truly understand and grasp what's in God's Word, is critical.

In Bible translation, we lay the stage for all the ministries that come behind us: for the planting of the local church, for discipleship, for all that comes next. To me, it's the first step of evangelism.

When I came onto the board, I thought I knew quite a bit about Bible translation. I really didn't. What I knew was the end result. But the process of getting there is difficult work. It takes a bright and capable person, and those people are speckled all over the globe.

My partnership with Seed Company has made me love Scripture more. I've had to step back and say, "Wow, this is really a gift that not everyone has." I've been encouraged to not take it for granted, to really love it, study it, and enjoy it. From a personal perspective, that has been quite special for me.

I love Seed Company. It's run like a business. We have goals, we have high expectations, and we have hard work. Those things are valued, and they really are accomplished. The board is full of people who are quite capable, and also quite fun. I have gotten to know different people and form some very special friendships, and our bond is with Scripture, so it's pretty awesome.

Through transitions, I have watched God give different leaders the skillset for what Seed Company needed at that time. It really encourages me that the company is on the right path, and that we need to go, go, go, get it done.

CHAPTER 2

IN THE CENTER OF THE SURGE

Before Katy Barnwell arrived in 1999, Seed Company was primarily a funding agency, with no direct field operations. Her transfer from SIL that year—to oversee the launch of the hugely influential Luke Partnership with The JESUS Film Project—changed everything and served to expand Seed Company's work into the hundreds of translation projects that the agency manages today.

Change usually comes slowly to organizations, especially mature ones.

Every so often, however, key trends and people collide to create what could be called a *flashformation*—a dramatic alteration that reforges a company's direction forever.

In June 1999, the entire Bible translation movement experienced a flashformation—one that gave everyone involved a brand new common goal and, in the process, utterly altered Seed Company's scope of operations.

SIL and Wycliffe Bible Translators had convened both of their international staffs in Waxhaw, North Carolina. For the two organizations, Vision 2025 was hitting delegates in a powerful way. What began as the caboose of the conference agenda

A group of people watches the "JESUS" film in Nigeria. Thanks in part to the Luke Partnership between Seed Company and The JESUS Film Project, the film is the most translated of all time, according to Guinness World Records.

Photo: Katherine Wells, courtesy of The JESUS Film Project

quickly came to drive it—the vision of translating Scripture for more than 3,000 totally unreached languages over the next 26 years. It was a huge shift, and one that guides Seed Company's thinking to this day.

While Vision 2025 was commanding the general conversation, Dr. Katy Barnwell had a personal change on her mind. Then a 35-year veteran translator, consultant, and trainer in Nigeria, Katy had been working as SIL's international translation coordinator for 10 years. She was looking for a fresh challenge.

For the two years leading up to the conference, Wycliffe USA President Roy Peterson and one of Katy's longtime friends, John Watters (SIL/Wycliffe Africa Area Director at that time), had been talking with Paul Eshleman, Director of The JESUS Film Project. (At the same time, Seed Company Founder Bernie May also was talking with Paul about partnering on the "JESUS" film.)

The JESUS Film Project depended entirely upon Wycliffe to do translations of the Gospel of Luke for its scripts. But there was no coordinated effort yet between the two organizations about language priorities.

Paul asked Roy if Wycliffe or SIL could translate Luke for his list of the top 30 languages that lacked the "JESUS" film. Roy explained that SIL and Wycliffe didn't work that way—they depended upon missionaries to choose the languages they translated. So Paul probed further: what would each Luke translation cost, and would SIL be willing to do them if The JESUS Film Project could raise the money? Roy said each one would cost about $100,000, and yes, SIL would do them if Paul could raise the $3 million. But who would run it? Leadership at SIL agreed that this new idea didn't fit well inside SIL, but might fit under Seed Company.

The catch: Seed Company wasn't doing field work in 1999. Up until then, Bernie and his small team primarily raised money for SIL-managed translation projects. But John noted at the time that Seed Company already had an innovation mentality about fundraising and empowering foreign partners to lead translation projects. All they needed was a point person.

Roy thought Katy was just the one. So did John.

So with Roy's blessing, John asked Katy if she would transfer from SIL, for whom she'd worked since 1964, to launch a new partnership with Seed Company and the "JESUS" film. Katy said yes, and in 2000 she helped to start work on the Luke Partnership, a joint effort of The JESUS Film Project and Seed Company.

The goal of the Luke Partnership was to begin Scripture translation in languages where there was none, beginning with the Gospel of Luke, followed by the "JESUS" film script. Instead of focusing on just one language at a time, they addressed clusters of related languages, often five or six at a time. Project facilitators held workshops to train translators from each of the languages. They involved local churches wherever possible in hopes that more Scripture translation could be done after the initial goals were met.

Paul explained:

> *It gave us hope and a way forward, because none of us were Bible translators. We were 100 percent dependent on Wycliffe. We'd have hundreds of missionaries and places in the world where they'd say, "It's so important. It's the best tool we could have not only to evangelize but to start churches. We desperately need this." When we signed the Luke Partnership agreement, suddenly Wycliffe was saying, "We will do this if you can provide the funds." It gave us a way. We could go after the funds and we could help those people who were so desperate.*

The original Vision 2025 resolution set the table for this new development. It read, in part:

> *Motivated by the pressing need for all peoples to have access to the Word of God in a language that speaks to their hearts, and reaffirming our historic values and our trust in God to accomplish the impossible, we embrace the vision that by the year 2025 a Bible translation project will be in progress for every people group that needs it. We acknowledge that this cannot be accomplished simply by our working harder or doing more of what we are now doing. It will require us to make significant changes in our attitudes and ways of working.*

According to Katy,

The focus was on partnership. It was at that time that the real focus on church and community involvement began to develop. This is not just a missionary task. ... There are many areas now, especially in Africa, where there is a growing church. The emphasis, all the way, needs to be on training others, both within the organization and with our national partners. People want to be trained. And as you see them coming in and taking the lead, you say, "Well, that's just wonderful. God prepared that person for that role." You see again and again that He has a pattern. He has a plan.

Peter Ochs

Peter Ochs was the first Chairman of the Seed Company Board of Directors and one of its original 10 financial partners. In 1976, he and his wife, Gail, founded First Fruit, a family foundation dedicated to supporting Christian organizations operating in the developing world.

A few years ago, we had a tremendous celebration at the first illumiNations event of having entered over 1,000 languages since the advent of Seed Company, suddenly taking an enormous bite into the remaining Bible translation needs of the world. As I look at that today, and I look at where the whole movement is, it's very exciting to see that we've probably moved up a hundred years from what was being projected back then as to when the last language would be entered—probably more than a hundred years, actually.

God's Word does change lives. It has powerful and almost mystical capacity. God speaks through His Word to people in our culture, in our language, and the same is true all over the world.

We have seen the power of God's Word to change lives. And yet at the same time, we've also been in many situations where we've been with people groups who don't have Scripture in their language and are dealing with Scripture in probably a national language, a local trade language. And we've seen firsthand how limited their understanding of that is. They don't get it. It's there, and they can sort of read the words. But reading the words and understanding what the words mean at the heart level are two very different things. And so, we believe that God will use His Word to bring people to Himself and to change their lives.

CHAPTER 3

LEADING BY LEAPS AND BOUNDS

Roy Peterson led Seed Company through its time of biggest growth.

It was about 5:30 a.m. in Orlando, Florida, and Wycliffe USA President Roy Peterson prayed hard as he walked through his neighborhood.

The year was 2002. Roy and his wife, Rita, had committed to a 40-day, liquid-only fast in order to devote themselves to fervent prayer. In particular, they prayed about Wycliffe's new headquarters opening in Florida and for a new chief executive officer to lead Wycliffe's 9-year-old affiliate, Seed Company. As Roy walked, he felt the Holy Spirit impress him that he was the next Seed Company CEO.

Convinced it was God leading him to a new challenge, Roy consulted Rita, close friends, and the Wycliffe and Seed Company boards. A short time later, he submitted his name for consideration.

When Roy accepted the call to lead Seed Company in 2003, the agency was engaged in 208 language projects. As he prepared to leave his decade-long run as CEO, the 1,000th translation project was started.

*Roy Peterson led Seed Company as President and CEO from 2003–
2013. When he took over, Seed Company had engaged with a little
more than 200 translation projects. When he left to join American
Bible Society, the agency had just taken on its 1,000th language.*

Photo: Rita Peterson

Under his leadership, Seed Company held steady in its mission: "To accelerate Scripture translation and impact for people without God's Word through Great Commission partnerships." A threefold impetus—speed, quality, and collaboration—guided everything the company did.

"Even though I was on the founding board for nearly six years, it took me awhile as CEO to understand how profoundly different—and what a change agent—Seed Company actually was," Roy said.

Seed Company cleared hurdles that weren't even in plain sight yet:

- Accelerating training of mother tongue translators to be consultants

- Developing the Luke Partnership with The JESUS Film Project

- Using Proclaimer audio devices for oral communities

- Implementing the BGAN satellite system to bring broadband access to remote areas

- Pioneering a crowdsourcing model in India that combined Scripture engagement and translation, while providing a way to measure community involvement

With a passion for God's Word that was contagious to Seed Company's staff, field partners, and translators, Roy led the company through a period of growth that he noted was clearly a work of God.

He also brought business development expertise. To familiarize high net worth financial partners to Seed Company's work, with the support of board member Todd Peterson, Roy initiated The President's Forum in 2008. The event ensured a steady stream of education and enthusiasm among financial and prayer partners.

The events served to bolster the quarterly updates that Seed Company was already writing to keep financial partners informed about the progress of translation projects. Roy gave ample credit to his mentor and friend, Seed Company Founder Bernie May, for recognizing and applying business savvy into Bible translation.

According to Roy,

> *The organizational difference between the for-profit world and the non-profit world is essentially zero. [Business consultant] Peter Drucker said that a business has only one purpose, and that's to cultivate and serve its customers. ... And in Bible translation, if you don't have a customer—if you don't have a financial partner—you can't do any Bible translation. There is no Bible translation without a target audience and resources, plus prayer. What Bernie understood was that if we do this well and we serve our financial partners well, we're going to be able to do more Bible translation ... because we'll have the resources.*

Roy's earlier overseas work with Wycliffe Bible Translators in Ecuador and Guatemala, plus two terms as President of Wycliffe USA, provided a springboard for partnership activity in the Bible translation movement. As Seed Company's President, he traveled, attended events, and participated in meetings that centered on global initiatives. His ever-growing network of colleagues helped the organization think and work smart.

As with many stories of God's work, Roy's began with his own salvation in 1973. He was a 19-year-old college dropout sequestered in a Mexican prison. Two English speaking inmates happened to be Christians and invited him to a Bible study. But the Bible was in Spanish. Graciously and tediously, they translated it for Roy as they studied.

Reticent at first to surrender his pride, Roy remembers when a troupe of Jesus People from Southern California held a worship service at the prison.

"The whole meeting, of course, was in Spanish, even the songs. But for some reason that day, it didn't matter," he wrote in his 2017 book, *Set Free: Unstoppable Hope for a World That is Waiting.*[1] "When the long-haired evangelists broke out their guitars and sang Scripture-filled songs, it seemed to me as though the universal language of love filled the room. The Holy Spirit rushed in. Peace washed over me."

He asked the Jesus People for an English Bible. They had none at the time, but they brought one to him the next time they came.

"It seemed I had to wait a long time to read God's Word in my own language," Roy said.

He never shook the feeling of waiting in darkness. Whenever he thought of Bibleless people in the world, the memory spurred him on, always with a sense of urgency. So, as a young businessman in the 1980s, he found himself more excited about Bible translation than his latest business deal in the greeting card business.

Going on staff with Wycliffe Bible Translators in 1986 seemed like a natural fit. He credits those years he and Rita spent in Ecuador and Guatemala with preparing him for his later leadership roles. Roy shared:

> I learned so much about Bible translation, living in context and getting to know the people. I got to know the mother tongue translators, and I also learned from the Western experts who were either translators themselves or consultants. And I grew in my understanding of the complexities. I saw how difficult Bible translation is and what a hard, long task it is.

When Roy took the helm of Seed Company in 2003, the agency already had met Founder Bernie May's goal of working in 200 languages by the time he retired in 2002. So when Roy came, he brought with him a vision, outlining an audacious goal: to reach 1,000 languages in 10 years. Roy shared,

> And that's exactly what happened. Every year, we kept growing, growing, growing the capacity, and God used that growth map. The vision became the foundation for making all kinds of decisions on fundraising, on staffing, all kinds of decisions, office space—everything was based on that 10-year plan.

With that victory, Roy sensed God leading once again and accepted an invitation to serve at the American Bible Society in 2014, where he and his staff continue to impact the Bible translation movement.

Never far from his mind is the Seed Company model he helped grow: connecting kingdom-minded investors to projects with which they could not only resonate, but also interact and minister.

And so everybody wins. The Seed Company wins, the financial partner wins, the translation project wins. The people group gets the Scriptures and everybody wins when you create a philanthropic-centered model.

Seed Company's legacy during Roy's tenure proves that: a decade with more Bible translation projects started than ever before. He calls it the greatest translation movement in all of Church history.

"We are watching God do it. What a privilege."

Footnote:
1. Roy Peterson, *Set Free: Unstoppable Hope for a World That is Waiting*, 2017, American Bible Society, Chapter 2.

Orville C. Rogers

Orville Rogers was born in 1917 on a ranch near Hubbard, Texas. He served in the U.S. Army Air Corps and then in the U.S. Air Force. He also served as a civilian pilot for 31 years. Orville has delivered missionary airplanes all over the world for JAARS and others. He counts SIL's and Wycliffe's Founder, the late William Cameron Townsend, and Seed Company Founder Bernie May as personal friends. Orville and his wife, Esther Beth (now deceased), were married in 1943 and have four children.

I met Uncle Cam Townsend in 1965. He challenged me to pick up the financial burden of a Helio Courier (airplane) that was ready to go but not funded. I did that, and then he asked me to ferry it to Bogota, Colombia. That was my first ferry flight for JAARS. There have been about 40 more since then, and I'm very, very grateful that God has given me that opportunity.

But after talking to Uncle Cam and realizing the challenge to Wycliffe Bible Translators, I realized that I had probably six, eight, or 10 Bibles in my home, and there were people groups all around the world that didn't have one word of God's book to use in their native tongue. And that got into me. I was introduced to Bible translation by aviation, but I've been challenged since then with the opportunity to help as much as I can with the task of reaching the Bibleless people of the world with God's Word.

The tremendous challenge of reaching out to the people groups of the world that don't have God's Word in their own language is a powerful, powerful motivator. And it's just a shame that it has taken us 2,000 years or more, and we're still not finished. I was hoping I'd live to see that day, but I don't think I will.

CHAPTER 4

NEW TECHNOLOGY, NEW POSSIBILITIES

Leveraging new technologies like satellite internet in hard-to-reach places helps accelerate Bible translation and transforms communities.

Mandowen, a young Yawa man in Southeast Asia, walked through the forest and saw a pile of gold sitting at the foot of a tree.

"Take the gold and give it to the people in your village," said a bird perched in a tree.

Mandowen put the gold in his bag, slung it over his back, and began his journey home. There was a man walking ahead of him whom he could barely see due to the thick fog. He followed the man back to the village.

Then, he woke up. He wasn't sure what this strange dream meant. Later that day, while Mandowen was in his garden, a little boy came running toward him.

"Mandowen, you have to come back to the village! There's someone here to talk with you."

That someone was Larry Jones, a Wycliffe missionary who was there to ask Mandowen to join the Bible translation team.

*Technology advances such as laptop computers and the Broadband
Global Access Network (BGAN) have helped hundreds of translators
in remote places connect with colleagues worldwide.*

Photo: Daniel Peckham

Years later, Mandowen tearfully told Larry that was the day he realized exactly what his dream meant.

"God had called me to bring the treasure of His Word to my people and said you would show me how to do it," he said.

By the time Mandowen joined Larry and his wife, Linda, the first portion of Scripture—the gospels of Matthew, Mark, and Luke—had been published and well received by the Yawa people. In 1992, the Joneses moved because of a change in assignment. Mandowen lived with them for a few years, but eventually returned to his village and his family.

Because he lived on a remote island with no electricity, telephones, or internet, sending timely manuscripts to Linda, the project consultant, was difficult. So they decided to meet in person for periodic consultant checks, requiring travel for both. Mandowen and other Yawas traveled up to six days one way on an overloaded ship, and were often sick by their arrival.

In 2008, shortly after Larry took on a new role with Seed Company, the agency's information technology department discovered a new technology called the Broadband Global Access Network (BGAN). This technology allowed people, like Mandowen, in remote places to connect to the internet by satellite.

In 2009, a satellite receiver and generator were installed. A laptop replaced Mandowen's typewriter, and he learned to use the new equipment to do final revisions of the Yawa New Testament so it could be published.

This pilot project wasn't flawless; at one point, when connection was lost, resolving the issue took months. Despite the glitch, BGAN accelerated the translation process by years and served as a model for future projects. Today, the BGAN technology is used globally, standing as a bridge between the treasure of Scripture and the Bibleless people in remote places.

In 2011, the Yawas celebrated the dedication of their New Testament. Mandowen cited 1 Corinthians 14:10, "There are many different languages in the world, and every language has meaning" (NLT). Mandowen cherished this verse because to him it meant that God values the Yawa language, and the Yawa people.

Today, Mandowen continues living out that dream of bringing treasure to his people. He's leading a team translating the Psalms, and the work already has transformed the way they worship through songs.

"The Yawas, like many people who speak minority languages, are at the lowest strata of their national society and economic system," Larry said. "They often are not perceived, and don't perceive themselves, as being very important or worth very much. Having Scripture in their language … has been enormously affirming."

Kent Bresee

Kent serves as a managing principal of Revayah Capital LLC. His love for Christ leads him to invest in companies to generate returns for investors while also supporting kingdom ministries. He has served as the American representative for the Business Professional Network Foundation and has been involved with making Scripture available in Africa since 2004. Kent has traveled the world extensively, having worked in Africa, China, and Switzerland, establishing significant networks along the way.

When I was in college, audio Bibles became available for free through biblegateway.com. That was the first time I had accessed the Bible in a way that really opened it up to me. I had struggled with different kinds of learning available in public schools, but I was a great auditory learner. Being able to listen to different versions of the Bible totally unlocked Scripture for me.

Because of my difficulty, I began to care about people who might have a Bible in a language or a form they care about, yet it isn't accessible like one in their own language would be. It made sense. If the tables were turned, I would want someone to care about Bible translation or availability for me, because God's Word opened my eyes. Hearing Scripture over and over again oriented my internal compass, and I want people to have that opportunity in their own language, too.

God's Word elevates societies. I saw that when we were helping bring the Bible into different places in Africa and India. We'd suddenly see relationships between men and women improve—certainly with husbands and wives. We'd see the relationship between people and their governments change. It opened the door for employers and employees to be different toward each other.

We want that for the whole world. The whole world needs the development that Jesus brings, and He's given that through the revelation of Scripture.

CHAPTER 5

PRAYING THE PROJECT THROUGH

For decades, missionaries and local Christians had puzzled over how to present the Gospel to Muslim people near the Chad/Sudan border. When a group of churches began to pray around the clock for a series of Bible storytelling workshops, Muslims who previously showed no interest in Christ began to enthusiastically share the stories with their families and neighbors.

The old man with the white beard looked agitated. As the sole representative of an all-Muslim people group in Chad, the elder had come willingly to the Bible storytelling workshop at the request of some other Chadians. He had one problem, however.

His people wanted nothing to do with Christians.

The first two-week workshop was held in eastern Chad in 2016. Three of the four largest people groups in the area sent representatives, but not the fourth. One local Christian piped up, saying he knew of a man who represented that group for the government—the elder with the white beard.

As Seed Company Field Coordinator Larry relayed it, on the first day of that first workshop, the elder pulled aside the project facilitator, Ahmed, and offered him a deal.

When Christians in Chad began praying for a series of workshops in a predominantly Muslim area, it turned a project that many believed would be a huge failure into a glowing success, said people involved with the project.

Photo: Jonathan McGuire

"I know exactly what you're doing here," the elder told Ahmed. "Let me tell you something—in my house I have a New Testament, and I read it. And I can't help you, because if I helped you, everybody would view me as a traitor. But I'll find some people who can help you."

The elder made good on his promise. He went back to his village and sent several young men to learn how to tell Bible stories to their people.

"If that guy had blown the whistle and started going to the mosque in [his town] saying, 'These people are here, trying to compromise our faith and take our young people away from us,' that workshop could've ended right there, even before it started," Larry said. "But somehow God helped them find the right guy."

But how? Larry would be the first to say that it was the prayers and financial support of local Chadian churches that helped turn the tide. And it started well before the idea of an Oral Bible Storytelling workshop was ever conceived.

Years ago, a well-known mission agency tried to do some translation work among the four people groups represented at the workshop. They made virtually zero headway. Ahmed, who grew up Muslim and came to faith in Christ through an American mission agency, visited those churches in 2014.

Workshop participants went home in the evenings and field-tested the stories with their families and friends. The next day, they'd come back and compare notes on what their focus groups said. After the workshop, one organizer reported that of the four language groups, the young men sent by the elder did better community testing than any of the others.

The incident with the elder was one more piece of evidence that a prayer initiative launched months earlier really had made the difference. One Chadian workshop attendee told Larry that without prayer, the work would be very difficult. What's more, he was uncertain of the workshop's success without it.

With prayer, however, the man had seen a lot of change in local people's hearts—as evidenced by several men who once attended the mosque now attended church on Sundays.

"We see these changes because God has their hearts," the Chadian man said. "This workshop will continue because the people are praying. It's not the technique [or] the work. It's the Word of God in the people."

In Chad, the cultural dividing line between north and south is even more pronounced than in the United States. The South is predominantly Christian while the North is majority Muslim. So even though many Northerners readily choose to follow Christ, the idea of becoming "southern" is anathema to them.

"So part of what we hope to do is to introduce people to Jesus—what it really means to be a follower of Christ—and let them develop communities of believers in their own context, in their own way," Larry said.

Larry marveled that a situation that drew so much pessimism at first, even from local Christians, could so quickly yield a series of positive workshops.

"Just the fact that the local churches in that community—even though they don't represent the same types of people groups—the fact that they're 100 percent on board, that they're doing what they can to help move things forward, I think is very significant," Larry said.

Rick Alvord

Rick Alvord is a founding Seed Company Board member. He is President and CEO of Powerstride Battery and Powerstride Golf Cars in Corona, California.

I think it's hard for us as Westerners to really grasp what it means to not have God's Word in our own language, because we grow up with so many Bibles in our homes, with so many translations.

My family is excited about Bible translation because we've witnessed what happens to a culture when God's Word comes to them for the very first time in their heart language. Imagine a place where God's Word isn't used to help make decisions, help define marriage, help us with our relationships, with how to raise our children. There are so many areas in which God's Word impacts our lives. It's not only the Gospel, but a blueprint for life.

Bernie May shared his heart with me about how important it was that Bibleless people had God's Word in their language, and how my company could be involved. I was called to be part of this because of Bernie, [because of] the desire to see Matthew 28 fulfilled, and because of the desire to see every Bibleless people group have God's Word in their own language. The fact that Seed Company was a start-up organization, and that it was going to be accelerating Bible translation, really appealed to my wife and me.

When my wife, Laura, and I decided that our company would sponsor the translation, we began to talk very openly with our kids so they'd understand why we were involved with Bible translation and what Seed Company was all about. As we received briefings from our project, we would take time at dinner to read the briefings and then pray for our translator. It became a big part of our family life.

In the earliest days, we weren't sure exactly how this was all going to work. It was very much an exploratory project to try to figure out what God was doing. It's amazing to see what God has done with a handful of people trying to accomplish the task of bringing God's Word to the Bibleless. I think about [the last] 25 years now of His blessing, His direction, and His guidance over this organization, and it's so clear that He's been leading this process.

Quizzical Moment, by Hyatt Moore

PART II

REACHING EACH HEART

CHAPTER 6

OPENING THE GATES FOR TRANSFORMATION

In some of the world's toughest places, people's first interaction with Scripture comes from oral Bible stories and the "JESUS" film in their heart language.

Picture more than 100 million people living in an area the size of Indiana. Ninety percent of those people live in 45,000 rural villages with populations less than 3,000 each. Access to education and healthcare is minimal. Crime is high.

That was Dev Bhoomi* in the 1990s. As a stronghold of Hinduism, Buddhism, Sikhism, and Jainism, Dev Bhoomi was not exactly fertile soil for the Gospel. The state was—and still is—less than 1 percent Christian.

"Missions were coming here and were unable to thrive because of the spiritual climate and because of the oppression that was here," said Luke*, a physician who has led a Christian outreach ministry since 1993.

"But God did something wonderful in Dev Bhoomi."

A group of women in South Asia listen to oral Bible stories on a portable audio device. Oral Bible stories have become a prime vehicle for introducing the Word of God to people living in areas of the world that are hard to reach because of religious, political, or geographic difficulties.

Photo: Michael Currier

Luke and his new wife, Lilah*, moved here in the mid 1990s. Their first night, they both had the same dream: a large group of poor, hungry children holding empty bowls and pleading, "Give us bread."

The couple believed God had spoken to them, but they were confused. This wasn't exactly what they had in mind when they came here. Then they realized: almost half of the state's population were children.

"So we started about 14 schools with about 3,000 children, and about 14 children's homes with about 450 children," Luke said. They also provided medical services.

While the work was helping thousands of children, Luke wasn't seeing a lot of spiritual impact in the region.

"I had made a mistake," he said. "I had thought that using the language of wider communication was enough. But we weren't seeing results. Not the kind that we see today."

What hadn't yet occurred to them as a priority was Scripture translation. Plenty of Bibles were available in Hindi, the area's widely spoken trade language. The region's few church services were conducted in Hindi also.

In October 2006, Luke's path intersected with that of Seed Company. Harry* and Jim* were touring South Asia to talk with church planters about Bible translation needs among indigenous people groups. They were also testing the relatively new idea that the first Bible stories a community receives should be chosen by the local people, based on their cultural needs. Prior to this meeting, the men had received little interest.

"What can we do to help you?" Harry asked Luke. Luke didn't know how to answer. *What is this man saying?* he thought. *There's nothing he can help me with. I live among very poor people. I live among illiterate people. Bible translation is for the highly educated, those who know computers and those who can give 10 or 15 years of their life to a highly academic discipline. That's not Dev Bhoomi. Dev Bhoomi is just the opposite.*

Harry saw Luke's hesitancy and asked, "Well, what language is spoken there?" Again, the question didn't resonate because Luke's ministry had been doing all of its work in Hindi, the trade language.

"Ganbi*," Luke replied. More than 700,000 people spoke Ganbi, one of six major languages in Dev Bhoomi.

Harry opened his laptop computer and typed Ganbi.

"And bingo, up comes Ganbi with four red stars," Luke remembered. That meant it was a top priority in the world. No oral Scriptures, no portions of Scripture, no "JESUS" film, no printed New Testament.

Luke thought of his trade-language approach and said, "I must be doing something wrong."

In 2007, Luke convened a meeting of a dozen Christian ministries (including Wycliffe). He still wasn't sure Bible translation had anything to do with the work in Dev Bhoomi, but he decided he could at least bring people together to talk about it. By the end of that conference, the group agreed on a first step for Dev Bhoomi—30 oral Bible stories in each of six languages, starting with Ganbi. Luke and others recruited mother tongue translators, and with the help of Seed Company and SIL, the work was checked rigorously for biblical accuracy.

Nine months later, in mid 2008, 106 teachers were sent out to the villages. The stories were being heard in mostly non-literate communities, both through listening groups and on Proclaimer devices.

The immediate impact was significant and wide-ranging. Luke breathed a thankful prayer: *God, this is Your timing for Dev Bhoomi.*

"We shared these Scriptures with pastors, and we told them, 'Please, serve your people in their own heart language, not the language of wider communication.' And as they started to use the Scriptures, hundreds of churches were planted because people understood for the first time that Jesus was speaking their language."

Then came August. Monsoon rains overwhelmed an earthen levee upriver, flooding hundreds of villages in Dev Bhoomi. Almost 3 million people were driven from their homes. Luke and Lilah opened their campus to several thousand refugees, providing food, clothing, and shelter.

With many on Luke's staff newly trained in telling Bible stories, they suddenly had an attentive audience. The stories proved popular and encouraging. Prayer groups sprung up. When the floodwaters receded, the people took those stories back to their villages.

Next came the translation of the Gospel of Luke, then production of the "JESUS" film, and then the entire New Testament in three languages—becoming the Seed Company project known as the Streamlands Cluster.

"This actually opened the gates for transformation and also for engagement with God's Word so people can read it and meditate on it," Luke said. "As a result of that, hundreds of worshipping groups are now using the Scriptures in their heart language."

The work expanded to states surrounding Dev Bhoomi: 12 more languages, then 18, then 24. Today, Luke's ministry is part of Bible translation work in 49 languages in seven states, with more than 1,500 churches taking part. Church leaders have taken ownership of the production, distribution, and advocacy.

And almost always, people are interacting first with oral Bible stories and the "JESUS" film.

"We are a culture that loves drama," Luke said. "And so this has been a phenomenal thing in churches. People now sing stories. They talk about stories. And then it becomes a focus in Bible study groups where people who are non-literate or belong to oral cultures can listen to a story and retell it."

To say Bible translation has transformed Dev Bhoomi would be a stretch; the state is still less than 1 percent Christian. Spiritual oppression and crime remain part of daily life for many. But there's a beachhead. Thousands have found new hope. Hundreds of new churches are using heart languages for all areas of ministry.

Luke still marvels at how it all started.

"We had been living in Dev Bhoomi for many years and had connections across the state," he said. "And God used those connections, plus the fact that we were eager for change, to bring around the beginning of something incredible—a new journey for Dev Bhoomi."

* Pseudonym

Bob Creson

Bob Creson, President and CEO of Wycliffe Bible Translators USA, has been involved in Bible translation for 34 years. Bob serves on the board of Wycliffe Global Alliance as well as on the board of Seed Company.

Scripture changes people's lives. I've had the opportunity to work in Cameroon, West Africa, and see firsthand the impact of translated Scripture. It's really quite amazing when you see people engage with Scriptures for the very first time. They may have been exposed to Scripture in another language, like French or English, but when they hear it in their mother tongue, it's very powerful. It's life-changing!

That truth is at the foundation of everything our partners at Seed Company do. They are dedicated to helping create the opportunity for people to engage with Scripture—sooner rather than later. They helped develop a model for Bible translation called Common Framework that accelerates the pace of Scripture translation. The focus of the acceleration is not so much on how quickly Scripture is translated, but on how quickly it becomes available to people in ways they can relate to, so that their lives can be transformed by it.

Seed Company has been amazingly generous in sharing what they have developed. As a result, Common Framework has now become the model used by many Bible translation agencies. Their generosity has contributed to a new level of partnership in which the agencies work together, minimizing duplication of efforts and maximizing investments of skills, time, and funds.

Together, we're on the verge of accomplishing Vision 2025—a translation project in progress for every people group needing it by 2025. It's an unprecedented period of acceleration of the pace of Bible translation, and an unprecedented opportunity to watch God at work in the heart languages of the world. We are stewards of this point in history, and I am grateful to work alongside Seed Company as we approach the goal—zero Bible translation needs, zero unreached people groups.

CHAPTER 7

ORAL TRANSLATION STRATEGIES

Translating heart language Scripture orally has become a major focal point for Bible translators worldwide, especially in heavily oral cultures like those in Cameroon.

Cameroonian educator Leonard Bolioki felt called to work in Bible translation after he read aloud the Easter story to a church congregation in the Yambetta language. After the service, several women asked where he found the story of a man who suffered so much for them. He told them it came from Scripture and that they had heard it every Holy Week in French for decades.

But this was the first time they had heard it spoken in their heart language. First Corinthians 14:9 says, "It's the same for you. If you speak to people in words they don't understand, how will they know what you are saying? You might as well be talking into empty space" (NLT).

Eighty percent of the world's people, including many who are literate, are primarily oral learners. That is true for much of Cameroon, which has a 71 percent literacy rate. Trey Sewell, a Seed Company field coordinator, thought an oral approach to

Marie and Leonard Bolioki share a commitment to Bible translation. Leonard is a Cameroonian educator who felt called to work in Bible translation after reading the Easter story to a church congregation in the Yambetta language.

Photo: Trey Sewell

Scripture translation would work well in Cameroon. The country's 24 million people speak about 280 different languages.

"History is passed down orally, and many languages are without an alphabet," Trey said. After eight years, through the use of 18 active projects, Cameroonians are learning to effectively craft and retell Bible stories in their mother tongues.

"Most of us grew up in a culture where our parents and grandparents taught us using stories, and those stories live with us right to this day," said Efi Tembon, Director of Cameroon Association for Bible Translation and Literacy (CABTAL). "We are very happy to see Seed Company come alongside us to help build our capacity ... to reach communities with the Scriptures in an oral way, in a way that really connects with the people."

Sometimes, the impact is immediate. At a church service in the Eastern Bantu region, a storyteller used the people's heart language to tell the story from Luke 1 of Mary and the angel Gabriel. When the storyteller finished, a young man came forward and confessed he'd been a marijuana smoker and a murderer. He accepted Christ and was later baptized.

In another church service in the village of Lus, a storyteller told about Elijah and the Prophets of Baal (1 Kings 18). One man immediately threw away his bag of charms, confessing that he had deceived people with enchantments. He vowed that from that day on he would serve God, because His power surpasses all powers on Earth and in Heaven.

For Zac Manyim, the oral strategies have been welcome and timely. Born into a Christian family, Zac made a commitment to "live for Him alone" when he was 17.

"Since that day, my passion for service has not stopped growing," Zac said. He is a Scripture-engagement coordinator for CABTAL and an oral consultant/facilitator intern with Seed Company. His internship duties include training story crafters in all Cameroon projects. Zac explains: "The Oral Bible Storytelling provides a 'foretaste' of the written translation. And when the community hears a Bible story in their own language, they say, 'Ah! This really seems good!'"

Michel Kenmogne

Michel Kenmogne has served as Executive Director of SIL International since 2016. As former head of the Cameroon Association for Bible Translation and Literacy (CABTAL), Michel is the first person from the Majority World to lead a North American-based Bible translation organization.

I realize that I've now invested the best part of my life in the ministry of Bible translation. Having quit a job with the government of Cameroon in 1996 to join what was back then the Wycliffe organization in Cameroon, I felt strongly compelled by the Lord that this ministry is essential to the whole existence of Christianity as a religion and as an institution. The enterprise of Christianity relies on translation.

Just think about it. What language did Jesus speak? Aramaic. And where do we find the source text of Christianity, of the New Testament message today? We find it in Greek, which tells us that the entire Christian faith relies on translation from Aramaic to Greek. And when we look at the history of the Church, whenever the Church has stopped doing translation and has felt that one language could serve all the needs of the people, after some time, the Church went astray. Bible translation is essential to the sustainability of the Christian faith.

It is my conviction that it is impossible to successfully share the Gospel and make disciples without having Scripture available in the languages—not only languages that people understand, but the languages that have shaped their values, beliefs, and worldviews.

Discipleship is about challenging our worldview—our belief systems and value systems—to conform to the Gospel. If Scripture does not come to us in the same language that has shaped our values, then it will be impossible to establish sound and mature believers in the Christian faith. Bible translation makes all that possible.

CHAPTER 8

SPEAKING TO THE OUTER REACHES

All over the world, Oral Bible Storytelling is paving the way for the Gospel and further Bible translation by presenting the Word of God in a form that people understand.

Oral Bible stories occupy a place all their own in the Bible translation toolbox. People with no previous access to Scripture often hear oral Bible stories before they ever see or hear a formal translation of Scripture in their heart language.

Starting with OneStory projects in 2004, Seed Company joined other agencies in what has blossomed into a worldwide Oral Bible Storytelling movement. In mainland Asia, Oral Bible Storytelling training began with one minority people group and spread rapidly to many languages and villages throughout the region.

One group, the Yobee*, sent five people for Oral Bible Storytelling training as part of a multi-language Seed Company workshop in 2014. The Yobee are a minority language group living in a mountainous area. The soil around Yobee villages makes poor farmland, so many Yobee people go to the nearest large city to scavenge trash for recycling. Even in a rapidly modernizing Asian country, they were still so isolated that they didn't have even one book of the Bible translated into their heart language.

In rural East Asia, workshop attendees who learn oral Bible stories and how to tell them are witnessing the power of God's Word firsthand when people suddenly hear it in their heart language. In one people group, about 2,000 people accepted Christ as Savior after hearing oral Bible stories, according to workshop facilitators working in the area.

Photo: Jim Stahl

But then they got oral Bible stories.

Because of those stories, more than 300 people have professed faith in Jesus, according to Lydia, a 30-year-old Yobee woman who attended that first Oral Bible Storytelling workshop in 2014. The Yobee now have several books of the Bible in their language, as well as the "JESUS" film. Lydia shared that,

> *Many people after listening to a story come to believe. Also, many people retell the story they have heard to other people they know. I do not know why people often want to accept Jesus after they have heard the story. I don't have the words to describe it, but I know that every story in the Bible is alive.*

Many have believed because they've experienced God's power personally. Joseph, another Yobee storyteller, told the story of Jesus healing a demon-possessed man to a middle-aged Yobee man who himself was demon-possessed. For eight years, the man had been weak, unable to work, and had lived in constant fear. Immediately after hearing the Bible story, the man put his faith in Jesus. The next morning, after a peaceful night's sleep, the man got baptized in the nearby river and reported that he was completely healed.

"Only when you use the people group's own dialect [or] language can you touch the people group's heart," Joseph said. "This is the charm and fascination of them hearing it in their own language."

In another minority people group in that part of the country, 2,000 people placed their faith in Christ after hearing oral Bible stories, said Arthur* and Marie*, co-organizers of the 2014 workshop. A traveling evangelist who goes by the initials JKS began telling Bible stories to people in a few villages he visited for the first time. Those people had never heard of Jesus and wondered aloud if He was a demon. They'd never heard of anyone else having that kind of power.

After a few months, JKS traveled to more villages a few valleys away. Instead of people mistaking Jesus for a demon, JKS heard questions like, "Is this Jesus the Son of God that we've been hearing about?"

"These stories had gotten legs of their own," Marie said. Arthur added,

> And, I like to say, [the stories] had been going over mountains and down through valleys into villages and into people's hearts. And they were impacting them deeply, giving them an alternative worldview that they'd never had to ponder before.

Spoken Bible stories have paved the way for the Gospel; this is a pattern that Arthur has seen all over that part of Asia:

> As I think about these stories being an introduction to the coming of the Word in the translated form, it made me think of the parallel that happened when the Messiah came. God didn't send the Word just outright, dropping it down to Earth. It didn't work that way. Rather, God brought John the Baptist first to prepare the way for the coming of the Word.

* Pseudonym

Dr. Bob Botsford

Dr. Bob Botsford is Senior Pastor of Horizon Christian Fellowship in Rancho Santa Fe, California.

At Horizon, when we roll something out, it's full band at full volume. It just flows out of our very DNA that way. We were in the midst of studying the Gospel of John, so I asked [Seed Company representative] Doug Wicks, "Who else needs the Gospel of John? We're studying it right now, but it seems a shame for us to study the Gospel of John for the nteenth time while there are parts and pockets around the world that have never read it once."

He came back to me and said, "I've got one for you. There's an island off the west coast of Africa called Annobon." I have a daughter named Anna and my wife is named Bonnie, so Annobon just seemed to resonate for some crazy reason. The island had a population of about 5,000 people, about the size of our church, so we just said, "We'll take Annobon, and we will put the Gospel of John in the Fa d'Ambu language."

By asking our congregation to sponsor one verse per individual or per family, we raised the money to cover every verse in the Gospel of John in one weekend. Doug was blown away. I was blown away. The church was head over heels with excitement for the opportunity. And so we felt like, *gosh, we got to that finish line too fast.* I was kind of looking forward to enjoying the race a little more.

So we rolled out another one, in an area that's called the graveyard of missionaries. The moment our church heard that the Bible was illegal there, they got more excited: "We get to do something illegal for Jesus!"

We sponsored that one in two or three weekends. Then, we did a third one in East Asia. We've got five orphanages over there so that one was an easy choice for us.

To whom much is given, much is required (Luke 12:48).

CHAPTER 9

MEETING PEOPLE WHERE THEY LIVE

Oral Bible Storytelling gives Christians new tools to reach their own people and introduce them to God's Word.

At 4 years old, Bargi still wasn't walking. She'd been ill with a cough since birth. A witch doctor suggested that, as a toddler, Bargi must have crawled over a pregnant snake and the snake had miscarried.

Her parents, Keo and Meilo, wondered if she was *mingi*—cursed. If so, Banna tribal beliefs were strict. If the sickness didn't kill Bargi, her family would have to do it. Social pressure is born out of fear that the cursed child will bring drought, famine, or disease.

That was before Almaz Gunzar heard about Bargi. The Bible storyteller and former healthcare worker walked the dusty road through her Ethiopian town of Key Afer, up the mountain path to the family's house. Keo told her they had no more money to spend on treating her daughter.

"Don't worry, I don't want any money," Almaz told them. "I'll pray for the girl in the name of Jesus."

Bible storyteller Almaz Gunzar has seen the power of God working firsthand among people in her tribe in Ethiopia, the Banna. "Often, the sick go to witch doctors and end up discouraged when they don't get better," Almaz said. "When I pray for them in Jesus' name, they are healed. Many see God's power."

Photo: Esther Havens

Keo welcomed the offer. The two women sat together as Almaz held the child, sang, and prayed.

Within a few days, Bargi's cough disappeared. Before long, she was walking. "God's Word and His Spirit are at work in tremendous ways among the witch doctors," Almaz said. "Often, the sick go to witch doctors and end up discouraged when they don't get better. When I pray for them in Jesus' name, they are healed. Many see God's power."

Referred to by National Geographic as "Africa's Last Frontier," the Omo River Valley in southwest Ethiopia is occupied by nine tribes who speak nine different languages. About 225,000 people populate the remote region. In 2013, the Ethiopia Kale Heywot Church (EKHC) and Seed Company implemented Oral Bible Storytelling to the Banna, Arbore, Tsamai, and Hamer tribes. It was the first project of its kind in the region, with more than 30 accurate Bible stories crafted in each of those four languages.

That's the introduction. Subsequent work includes the "JESUS" film, the Gospel of Luke, and the full New Testament. Future success will be measured by increased understanding of Scripture, people coming to Christ, and the number of newly planted churches.

But success is already being measured from the stories of people like Almaz, whose heart already beat for sharing Christ with her people and who now has new tools to do that. She began sharing the Gospel during home visits as a government health worker a few years back, teaching women about pregnancy, childcare, sanitation, family planning, and other concerns.

She remembers meeting missionaries living among the Banna people—her people. *These people are passionate about the spiritual lives of the people whom they don't know,* she thought. *I am the only one in my family who finished my education.*

I know my people. Why don't I serve them this way?

Almaz's late father was the first Christian in Key Afer, led to Christ by missionaries. The seventh of nine children, Almaz grew up knowing about Jesus. But she didn't see faith outside of her own family until she worked with other Christians for the government health service. They were lively people, deeply committed to Christ. She wanted to be like them.

"I believed in God, but I hadn't determined to live for Jesus," Almaz said. Over the next six years, she dedicated her life's work to God.

Later, she resigned from her government position and began working full time in women's ministry at the local church.

"First, God changed my life and grew my faith," she said. "Now, God is doing something new for the Banna people."

When an opportunity arose to learn Oral Bible Storytelling through a Seed Company and EKHC workshop, Almaz went to the town of Arba Minch for training. As a result, today she travels the region, sharing Bible stories with the Banna as they plow the fields, walk on the road, shop at the market, or ride the bus.

"When people hear accurate Bible stories in their own language, the ideas are clear," she said. "They understand."

The first thing Almaz does when she enters a community is find a man or woman of peace. She sits with those who will listen, drinks coffee with them, and shares her life story and God's stories. "The Banna people relate especially to the themes of forgiveness, conflict, sin, and the schemes of Satan," she said.

Although Bargi's parents aren't believers yet, they have opened their house as a home of peace. Almaz and others meet there regularly.

As listening groups grow, house churches sprout. According to Almaz,

> It's as if God has opened the skies and made the community ready to receive the Good News. When I tell stories, others are positive and open to Christianity. Many are coming to Christ and their lives are changing. I'm not doing a hard thing. They are God's stories; I just tell them. … The ideas are simple to understand and they're learning to apply God's truths to their lives.

Today, Almaz serves as a trainer in a second Oral Bible Storytelling project focused on women, again sponsored by EKHC and Seed Company. She's helping train 25 women from southern Ethiopia to tell 40 stories about God's care, concern, and provision for women. The women tell stories in their local communities and plan to equip 500 more women to share accurate Bible stories.

Mark Taylor

Mark Taylor is President and CEO of Tyndale House Publishers. His father, Ken, was Founder of Tyndale House and creator of The Living Bible. Ken made the first major donation to Seed Company in 1993, with a gift of $100,000 a year for five years. Tyndale House donates a portion of proceeds from the New Living Translation—the update of The Living Bible, in which Mark played a leading role—to Bible translation through Wycliffe USA. The Tyndale House Foundation that Mark's parents established continues to support Seed Company.

At Tyndale, we start with the underlying premise that the Bible is indeed the Word of God for all people. But if it's not in your language, then it's not very accessible. And if it's in a translation—even if it is your own language—that you don't readily understand, then that's also not very accessible. We have always been motivated to see the Bible get into people's heart language, and that it be done in a way that allows people to read it and say, "I understand this."

Back in 1996, Tyndale proposed a five-year agreement where Wycliffe USA would receive contributions based on sales revenue from all New Living Translations. Here it is 20 years later and we're still doing that. Similarly, Tyndale House Foundation, which is our sister corporation, has been supportive of Seed Company from day one.

Wycliffe is doing things that we cannot do. Wycliffe is set up with hundreds of members around the world to reach into hundreds of languages, while we are focusing on English and Spanish. And then we support a number of translations. We simply see our support of Wycliffe as one way of taking the financial resources that we get from the English NLT and sharing it with smaller language groups around the world.

CHAPTER 10

THE LAST FRONTIER

Sign languages are among the last to be targeted for Bible translation. But the work is accelerating quickly.

The problem was clear.

The countdown for Vision 2025—with a Bible translation project started in every waiting language—was down to 10 years. Representatives from leading Bible agencies were meeting in Orlando, Florida, and the discussion steered to the challenges for sign languages.

Of more than 350 sign languages that need translation, none had a full Bible. American Sign Language (ASL) had the only full New Testament, with the Old Testament in the works. Until completion of the ASL Bible, there would be no source text for other sign languages.

Based on current funding and team structures, the Deaf ministries in attendance reported that the ASL Bible would be completed after 2030. That news jeopardized Vision 2025.

The translation agency leaders asked, "What do you need?"

There are more than 70 million Deaf people worldwide. Through D3 Vision 2020, Seed Company is one of just a few hearing Bible translation agencies providing funding for translations to reach the Deaf community.

Photo: Sandy Easton

Deaf Bible Society President J.R. Bucklew answered, "We need money so we can expand our teams."

"Okay," came the reply.

The result was D3 Vision 2020, allowing for more translation teams that would accelerate the timetable for the first full sign language Bible by more than a decade. D3 stands for the project's three primary field partners: Deaf Missions, D.O.O.R. International, and Deaf Bible Society. Seed Company is among the handful of "hearing" translation agencies providing funds to reach the long-neglected Deaf community.

There are more than 70 million Deaf people worldwide. Only 2 percent have been exposed to the Gospel. Not one has a full Bible in his or her heart language.

Sign language has been considered the last frontier for Bible translation. Its challenges are among the greatest in fulfilling Vision 2025. It requires more steps than other types of translation, increasing the cost. Security risks are inherent. The risks for people signing the Gospel on video in some parts of the world require employing developing technology such as motion capture and animation.

In 2017, Seed Company began building a research lab to devise faster ways to translate Scripture. This included working with an international expert in combining artificial intelligence with neuroscience research. The goal: produce breakthrough technology. Whatever the avenue, Seed Company is seeking solutions to accelerate projects like D3 Vision 2020.

Early impact would be completion of a book-by-book ASL Bible by 2020, which would serve as a source text—a cornerstone—for future sign language translations. The project also included an effort to engage more than 250,000 Deaf people in the United States with the Gospel in their heart language.

The Bible translation movement was not alone in being slow to recognize the distinctiveness and importance of sign languages. From 2010–2016, at least eight nations designated a sign language as an official language.

"A lot has changed in the last 10 years," J.R. said.

However, in some countries, deafness is still considered a form of demon possession, a curse on a home, or punishment for sin. And Deaf people bear scars from churches that claimed they are Deaf because they lack faith, or that faith comes only by hearing.

Imagine being surrounded by those beliefs and not having access to the truth of God's Word.

That truth is on the way, however, with the accelerated completion of the ASL Bible. With that comes the hope that every Deaf language in the world will have translation underway by 2025. J.R. adds,

> *None of us were around for the first printing of the Bible. Some were around for the first recording of an audio Bible. But most of us weren't around for some of those firsts. We have the opportunity, not just in our generation, but in the next couple of years to be part of seeing a first: the world's first complete Bible in any sign language.*

And for the Deaf, there is much more to come beyond that.

David Wills

David Wills is President Emeritus of National Christian Foundation, created in 1982 to work with donors who desire to advance Christian nonprofits. NCF is the world's largest Christian grant-making foundation, and David was introduced to Seed Company through his leadership there.

God's Word is a priority to me because it is a priority to Him. God's Word is the foundation for all of the ministry in the Church and all of the ministry that happens in the lives of those around us. I think we take the Bible for granted in America and other places where we've had free and uninhibited access to the text.

As someone who begins every day in God's Word, it is hard to imagine someone coming to me and saying, "You can't do that anymore, and you no longer have access to this book." That would make a dramatic impact on my life as a Christian and as a person—not to mention the lives of those whose paths I cross every day.

My first encounter with Bible translation was through Seed Company. Learning about the importance of Scripture translation endeared Scripture to me. Suddenly, the Bible went from a book that was taken for granted to something that was a precious gift, a valuable possession—something to be stewarded.

I have always been thankful for the Bible, but Bible poverty is like any poverty. When you experience and understand any form of poverty, it causes you to thank God for what He has given you in a way that you wouldn't have previously done. The more that I spend time working on the issue of Scripture translation, the more grateful I am that I have God's Word.

I'm part of a small group of guys—all of us are involved with Seed Company— and every morning, we read a chapter from the Bible and text each other a couple of thoughts from that chapter. We recently read Matthew 13, which recounts the Parable of the Sower. In that passage, Jesus explained how the Word falls on different types of soil. But that presumes that the Word is there to begin with.

If it's not even there, where is the seed that needs to be sown? Eradicating Bible poverty has to be at the top of the list of what we're charged to do because it's the foundation of all other ministry activities.

CHAPTER 11

NOT ALONE AND NOT FORGOTTEN

Sign language translation brings the hope of the Gospel to people who felt forgotten.

Carlos Silva believed he was the only Deaf child in the world. His family was poor. Amid the stunning beauty of Rio de Janeiro, a city that tourists came from across the world to enjoy, Carlos grew up ashamed of his surroundings.

Both parents were Deaf and illiterate. To put food in the often-bare cupboards, Carlos' father sold whatever items he could on the streets. His mother became a prostitute—working out of their one-room family home while her three kids were there.

"I was a poor kid, and I had no value," Carlos said. "And it was almost like I was garbage."

Now, as an adult, a seminary graduate, and a pastor, Carlos is part of the first sign language Bible translation project aimed at children.

He wants to help Brazil's Deaf children because he had no help during his childhood.

Seed Company joined the LIBRAS (an acronym for *Língua Brasileira de Sinais*) project in 2013, partnering with the Brazilian Bible Society, SIL, Brazil's IES (Deaf

Carlos Silva shares a moment with his daughter, Isadora. Carlos is part of the LIBRAS project in Brazil, the first sign language Bible translation project designed especially for children. The LIBRAS team hopes to produce a DVD set of 24 sign language Bible stories for children and the Book of Mark on DVD for adults.

Photo: Matt Knisely

Expression Institute), and Wycliffe Associates. The initial goals included a DVD set of 24 Bible stories for children and the Book of Mark on DVD for adults.

The children's emphasis came because of sects distributing materials to children in Brazilian Sign Language. Local churches and Christian schools needed evangelical resources of their own. The project would also help children improve their language skills.

At 40, Carlos has become a face of that project as a signer on DVDs and an advocate for Deaf Bible translation. He doesn't need to leave home to understand its significance.

In 2000, his wife, Fabiana, gave birth to a hearing son, Isaac. Twelve years later, their daughter, Isadora, was born.

"We discovered she was Deaf," Carlos said. "I kind of had a moment where I remembered how hard it was for me as a Deaf person."

Carlos recalled all the barriers he had faced in society, and knowing nothing about the Bible. He considered his time growing up as time lost.

He felt a heavy responsibility to do everything he could to help his Deaf daughter, on top of his commitment to spreading the Gospel to the 3 million LIBRAS users.

In April 2017, Carlos accepted an offer from IES to sign a Bible story in LIBRAS. Upon arriving for the assignment, he learned that his story was for children. He immediately thought of his 5-year-old daughter, envisioning Isadora learning Bible stories in her language.

When he brought the first DVD home, he and Isadora watched it together. Afterward, Carlos asked questions based on the stories, and she answered every one.

"I realized that she had understood everything," he said. "That translation is so important."

As a pastor, Carlos had seen little teaching for Deaf children in churches. He said it was almost as if the church had forgotten about them.

The LIBRAS project has changed that. The man who once thought he was the world's only Deaf child is helping introduce young, Deaf Brazilians to Jesus. And they're learning not only that Jesus knows they exist, but that He also wants to be their friend.

"I was just like them," Carlos said. "I know their parents were probably like mine. I've been able to learn. I've been able to develop as a person. And so I just think I need to love them. I need to help them."

Robby Moser

Robby Moser, a Seed Company Board member, is President and CEO of Clark Construction Group LLC, headquartered in Bethesda, Maryland. Among many high-profile construction projects, his company built the Museum of the Bible in Washington, D.C. Robby and his wife, Katy, live in Virginia with their sons.

We've been a part of local churches for many years. We supported local missions and then graduated to international support of missions. We always questioned how we were following the Lord's calling. Then, at a Seed Company event, God moved our hearts in a mighty way to the belief that Bible translation is what's required to fulfill the Great Commission. It changed our perspective to understand that there are men, women, and children around the world who can't enjoy the full richness of the Word of the Lord in their heart language. That compelled us to do something, to make a difference.

Missions we had supported in the past involved health and welfare of people— water wells, food, education. Those are critical missions, and we're delighted to know that brothers and sisters in Christ are supporting those. But we often found ourselves wondering, *How does that work if the people group doesn't have the Scripture in their language? How do they understand where this is coming from?*

I have the pleasure of being the CEO of a privately held company that's 110 years old. We plan for the long term. I see Bible translation as not for the faint of heart. It's not for those who want to see instantaneous results. But amazing results come. There's nothing better than the Word of the Lord in someone's heart language.

Actions are only as good as the energy you have in your body, but God's Word moves people. It moves nations. The physical well will run dry. A container of food may not come, but nobody can take the Word away from someone after it's in his or her heart language.

When a translator sits at your kitchen table, and he's talking about his kids who are your kids' ages, and about what they're doing, you see your kids' eyes get big. You hear about the risks they take, to move from location to location under the threat of persecution. This is no longer on the 11 o'clock news. This is real.

Supreme Joy, by Hyatt Moore

PART III

RESTORING EACH COMMUNITY

CHAPTER 12

AN UNLIKELY CALLING

Locally owned and managed projects are awakening abilities and callings the translators never knew they had.

In the center of Hlinné, Slovakia, stands a statue of Cyril and Methodius, the ninth-century brothers who first translated Scripture for the Slavic people. Just around the corner, their spiritual descendants set up wooden tables, laptop computers, and a coffeemaker, then set about translating the Old Testament into the local Romani language.

Roma people have been in Slovakia for 1,000 years, but they remain marginalized due to where they live and the languages they speak. In this village, East Slovak Romani (also called Carpathian Romani) is not only the language of everyday life, but for Christians it's also the language of prayer and worship.

Today, people carry both the East Slovak Romani New Testament (finished in 2014) and the full Slovak Bible to church. But the day is coming when eastern Slovakia's Roma believers will have the whole Bible in their heart language. Seed Company is partnering with The Word For The World on the Old Testament project.

Stano Tancoš (right) and his team work on translating the Old Testament into their heart language, East Slovak Romani.

Photo: Esther Havens

Here in Hlinné, the translation team works inside what was once a family home, which now hosts a vibrant Roma church. Someday soon, a local pastor will stand in this very spot and preach from the Scripture that the team is now translating. What's more, the project's success is spurring interest in translation among other Roma groups in Eurasia.

This astonishes the three men who once felt like the least-qualified Bible translators on Earth. Stano Tancoš recalled the day that he and fellow translators Pavol Godla and Miró Mitáč reached 1 Samuel 16, the story of David's anointing as king.

"We came to a standstill," Stano said. "It really touched us. God doesn't look at what a person looks like or their abilities, but He looks at the heart. It's a very powerful word."

None of the men graduated high school (a Roma cultural norm that's only now beginning to change). But for the team's project manager and translation adviser, Pierre van Vuuren of The Word For The World, character trumps paper credentials. From his involvement with several Roma churches in the area, Pierre knows Stano, Pavol, and Miró as intelligent men who love God—qualities needed to translate Scripture for their people.

The team typically works through 25 verses a day. Pavol uploads each translator's individual work into the Paratext computer program. The three Roma men talk through each verse, debating changes that would make the translation read more naturally.

Once they agree on the wording of a passage, Pierre checks it for accuracy against the Slovak and original Hebrew texts. A Bible translation consultant will eventually review their work and give approval for publication or recommend additional changes.

Several people have told Stano what it felt like to hold their New Testament for the first time. At first, they felt shame in seeing God's Word in what was viewed as a second-class language. But the shame was eclipsed by joy.

"I believe that they're not ashamed of their language anymore," Stano said as he looked up a word in the dictionary. "They have tasted of something, like myself, that we have God's Word in our language. That's something wonderful."

Pavol looked up from his screen.

"For our nation, for our people, this is something that is very precious."

Michael Stoltzfus

Michael Stoltzfus is President and CEO of Dynamic Aviation, Inc. A graduate of Harvard Business School, he is a third-generation supporter of Bible translation, following in the footsteps of his grandfather, Chris, and father, Karl. He also served on the Seed Company Board of Directors for nine years. A former agnostic, Michael has been involved in funding Bible translation projects for 20 years, including Scripture for the Nanti people of southern Peru.

The ability to have access to Scripture in my own mother tongue is central to my walk with Jesus. And it's one of the four [Jesus-centered] things I try to do on a daily basis. It's that important.

The Nanti [are a group of] a thousand people down in the jungles of southern Peru. Without someone stepping up to fund this, they're going to go through their life like I was when I was agnostic. And they're going to want to do the right thing, but they're going to have no model. They're going to have no relationship with Jesus. But the fact that I could be involved and allow them to have something life-giving, like I personally experienced, in their mother tongue, and grow in their walk and in their faith and in their love for Jesus and their love for one another—sign me up!

CHAPTER 13

FROM TRAUMATIZED TO TRANSFORMED

As God's Word reaches traumatized people, God transforms lives and brings healing.

The new boat hit dry land on Mfangano Island, carrying copies of the Suba New Testament. Suba men lifted the colorful boat, carrying it as they danced in celebration. Naphtaly Mattah, one of the translation project leaders, joined in the dancing alongside the men, women, and children.

"What a day of celebration that was," Naphtaly said, reflecting on the Suba New Testament dedication in 2011. "It was like Heaven literally came down amongst us."

For generations, Mfangano Island in southwestern Kenya was not a place of celebration. Canoes, an integral part of life on Lake Victoria, carried the memory of a dark ancestral tradition. The Suba required a human sacrifice to make a boat. The chosen tree would fall on a person, often someone elderly and isolated, and crush him to death. The Suba used the wood from that tree to make the keel, the most important part of the boat. They believed this practice led to canoes having spirits.

Translation project leader Naphtaly Mattah fondly recalled the Suba New Testament dedication. "What a day of celebration that was," he said. "It was like Heaven literally came down amongst us."

Photo: Seed Company

Outsiders considered the island cursed and full of witches, Naphtaly said. Government officials and missionaries avoided working there. Visitors feared becoming sick or being robbed, and finding a safe place to stay was difficult.

Sexual licentiousness in this fishing community contributed to the rapid spread of HIV/AIDS. In the mid-1990s, a report said that six out of 10 Suba mothers giving birth were HIV-positive—the worst rate in Kenya. Thousands of children were orphaned.

To make matters even worse for the Suba, they were losing their culture and language. Their identity had been wrapped up in the Luo people since the mid-1700s, when the Luo colonized and began to rule over the Suba. For a long time, Bible translation organizations assumed that the Luo Bible was sufficient for the Suba people. A survey even concluded that the Suba language was dying.

But some church leaders disagreed. They formed a translation committee and approached Kenya's Bible Translation and Literacy organization, requesting the New Testament in the Suba language.

Naphtaly was one of those church leaders.

In response to the translation committee's request, the organization started the Suba translation project in 1992 and appointed Naphtaly as the project leader. Shortly after, Seed Company partnered with the Suba as one of its first 10 projects.

While Naphtaly worked as a translator, he was impacted by the verse that says, "Pure and genuine religion in the sight of God the Father means caring for orphans and widows in their distress" (James 1:27a, NLT).

Naphtaly and his wife, Nereah, began welcoming orphaned children into their home. They eventually founded Gethsemane Garden Christian Center, primarily for HIV/ AIDS orphans. Because of this, hundreds of children who once lived on the streets received an education.

"God has enabled them to not only excel in academics and professions, but to excel in faith and to shine," Naphtaly said. "People see them and see what God alone can do." On visits to their extended families, many of these young evangelists led their family members to Christ.

Naphtaly was appointed county executive for education and has had the opportunity to reach schools across Kenya with the Gospel. In Naphtaly's region, the Evangelical

Church has grown from less than 100 people to thousands. The Old Testament is being translated into the Suba language as another Seed Company-backed project.

As God's Word is being taught and received by the Suba, HIV/AIDS has decreased by more than 20 percent. Medical treatment, clean water, and education are becoming more accessible. Tourists now flock to Mfangano Island and missionaries from the island are taking God's Word to other parts of Kenya.

Today, the Suba and Luo people intermingle and worship together as Christians on Mfangano Island.

"God has changed it from a cursed land to a land of healing," Naphtaly said.

When preparing for the New Testament dedication, the translation committee wanted the copies to be brought on a new boat. What once represented death now delivered the living Word of God.

"We were under such bondage to our ancestors," Naphtaly said. "Christ showed us that there was a new sacrifice. ... The boat has been important to us, but the wood on the keel is not as important as the wood on the cross."

PARTNER PERSPECTIVE

Jason Baker

Jason Baker is a retail broker/developer and Vice Chairman of Seed Company's Board of Directors. He and his wife, Susannah, first partnered with Bible translation in 2008, after a friend told them, "You guys need to get involved with Seed Company." Jason, Susannah, and their four daughters attend First Baptist Church in Houston.

I think back over our years with Seed Company, and we have developed amazing friendships with people whose hearts we have connected with through Bible translation.

Being involved in Bible translation has also changed the perspectives of our children, who have had the opportunity to be here when we have hosted a translator in our home. They've raised money through a lemonade stand ..., so they could give dollars and nickels to Seed Company. They've attended meetings with staff. They've met the people who are working in the field and they've met partner [organizations]. They have seen the measurable impact of God's Word.

We adopted a sweet baby girl from China almost two years ago, and it has been awesome to see our other three girls ... talk about getting older and doing life. The idea of adoption to them seems very normal. To me, it's the same with Bible translation and having a heart for God's Word. We talk about generosity toward Bible translation, about partnering, about the impact of God's Word.

Being involved in Bible translation has permeated every part of what we do and how we move on in life as a family. It affects our prayer life. It affects our family giving. It affects what we talk about. And it's really helped develop in our children—and in us as parents—a better global understanding of how God is moving.

CHAPTER 14

RESTORING HOPE AND DIGNITY

In two cultures where women have been oppressed, God is restoring dignity and hope through a Bible storytelling project.

"It appears that more girls have been killed in the last 50 years, precisely because they were girls, than men were killed in all the wars of the 20th century."[1]

As Dr. Larry Jones, Seed Company's Senior Vice President of Bible translation, turned the pages of Nicholas Kristof and Sheryl WuDunn's 2010 book, *Half the Sky*, he felt the need to act.

Larry, a husband and father, couldn't ignore the oppression and injustice suffered by millions of women each day. Education, economic equality, and adequate medical care top the list of investments that produce change.

"But what can a Bible translator do?" he wondered.

Halfway around the globe, physician and ministry director Luke* sat at his desk looking out his office window in rural South Asia. A crowd scurried up the dirt road carrying a 3-year-old girl clinging to life.

The Esther Project was formulated to serve and encourage women in South Asia by translating key Bible stories, including the book of Ruth, in their heart languages.

Photo: Jim Stahl

"When they found her, they brought her to the hospital," Luke said. "What I discovered was worse than anything I could have imagined." A drunken man had violated her in the night and left her for dead in the woods.

Later, when a government official asked whether Luke had heard about the girl and then commented on the trouble women cause, Luke was taken aback. "It was then that I began to realize the great extent of the lack of dignity for women and girls in this region," he said.

A phone call to an acquaintance and healthcare champion Dr. Margaret* helped shape the project. Together, these three imagined an Oral Bible Storytelling project focused on women—by women, for women. Seed Company partnered with a local ministry for the Esther Project, targeting unchurched and illiterate women in a particular state.

"A mother feeding a child and children playing are usually normal sights," Margaret said. Instead, in the country's poorest region, she sees unhealthy children with runny noses and mothers with blank, hopeless faces. Many live unacquainted with hope and resigned to fate.

The storytelling pilot project launched in 2014 with 23 marginalized women from different language groups, castes, and ethnic backgrounds. The first workshop was more than a little difficult.

"When I met these ladies, they were so timid. It took at least a half an hour before they started talking," Margaret said. "I had the impression they were hindered by customs, communities, community practices, and other social limits."

During the next two years, the women crafted 40 Bible stories and learned the Book of Ruth. They told accurate Bible stories in their own languages during church services, in personal evangelism, and in home gatherings. They ate together and prayed together. Over time, they grew in love and respect for one another. They learned that God loves women, even women whose common ties spurned them. Within two years, the women began more than 200 weekly listening groups, reaching more than 2,100 people. As the women prayed, many were healed.

Hundreds more found new hope.

"Today, I see how confident the Esther women are," Margaret said. "They are completely changed. Completely changed."

The women radiate courage, faith, and confidence because they've witnessed God's power everywhere they've shared stories. A withered hand is healed, evil spirits are banished, demons are dispelled, unwanted babies are delivered, marriages are reconciled, shame is dissolved, dignity is bestowed, beatings are ceased, mothers-in-law and daughters-in-law are united, derelicts are sobered, pain is eased, injustice is blocked, hope is tasted, promises are believed, and families are redeemed.

Seed Company encourages Bible translation partners to incorporate both oral and written strategies. When literacy rates are low, Oral Bible Storytelling provides an alternative avenue for the word. The response and application of biblical truth is immediate and can lead to dramatic change. As technology advances, people have access to hand-held audio players, cell phones, and radio broadcasts. They can also listen to stories again and again, multiplying the effect.

In 2016, a second Esther Project began in a remote part of Ethiopia where women are often ranked just above cattle in value. Twenty-five women tell Bible stories in the churches, hospitals, home gatherings, and prisons. They've trained 70 male prisoners to tell stories, and their goal is to train at least 500 women. As an early result, hundreds of Ethiopian women have found new hope.

"Women all over the world are [often viewed as] second-class citizens," Margaret said, "but in the Bible, I don't see Jesus treating women [as] inferior to men. In fact, He gives them special attention. The Esther Project, in one sentence, is for the purpose of empowering women for the Lord's work."

* Pseudonym

Footnote:
1. Kristof, Nicholas D. WuDunn, Sheryl: *Half the Sky* (Kindle Location 144–145). 2008, Knopf Doubleday Publishing Group. Kindle Edition.

Matt Mancinelli

Matt Mancinelli is a Seed Company Board member. For nine years, he worked for Generous Giving in Orlando, Florida, an organization that works with high-net-worth Christians to help them wisely steward their money. In 2017, Matt and his wife, Loretta, moved to Detroit, where Matt became CEO of Soar Detroit, a nonprofit that uses literacy, sports, and camps to help kids flourish.

Our lives have been shaped by and transformed by the Gospel, which has come through our interaction with the Bible. When we think of so many people and languages that still don't have any Scripture ... we see translation as a starting point, as the critical first step toward almost anything else that we can do anywhere.

There's a group of college friends that I've been getting together with for about 15 years. That group is one of a couple groups we started that is [partnering with] a translation. There are five of us involved in the project, and we each gave for the last few years. And it's been so fun to be on mission together. It hasn't been a withdrawal, like I might have imagined when I think of asking friends for money. It's been a deposit of something that we can all do together.

CHAPTER 15

SCRIPTURE HELPS TO HEAL TRAUMA

In war-torn countries, God is meeting people at their point of greatest need. He is using His Word to heal wounds through trauma healing workshops.

When the soldiers suddenly stopped their vehicle in front of Euphrasie Guerekon* and told her to get in, she ran. But like so many women who live surrounded by violence, she was not able to outrun the horrors of war.

The soldiers were part of the coalition that overthrew the government of Central African Republic (CAR) in March 2013. They took Euphrasie and drove her to their leader, who tried to make her his wife. When she refused, he raped her—as did the two soldiers who drove her home after the leader sent her away.

For people in war-torn countries, the reality of suffering can lead to isolation. Jesus prioritized serving outcasts and used stories to reveal the powerful narrative of his restoring love. In partnerships with national translators and organizations like American Bible Society (ABS), Seed Company has been using Scripture in story-based trauma healing workshops for women like Euphrasie since 2011. In fact, she attended a workshop in Bangui, the capital of CAR. The workshop was conducted in

Trauma healing workshops in Central African Republic and other African countries introduce Bible stories and biblical truth to victims of war trauma.

Photo: Galen Johnson

the local Sango language—Euphrasie's mother tongue—and led by ACATBA, a Seed Company partner and member of the Wycliffe Global Alliance.

The workshop in CAR used the book *Healing the Wounds of Trauma*[1] as its curriculum. Published by ABS in 2002, the book has been translated into many languages, making it a versatile resource for communities impacted by conflict. "Hearing Bible stories in the mother tongue allows young and old to engage the story and share their own experience freely," said Galen Johnson, who helped lead the workshop and is the Seed Company field coordinator for CAR and Democratic Republic of Congo.

Healing the Wounds of Trauma uses candid, modern-day narratives and Bible stories. It puts Scripture passages to song to help workshop attendees cope with painful experiences and teaches them how to share the Bible stories with others. The workshop's lessons are especially poignant for CAR, which has been brutalized by civil war, mass killing, and widespread rape.

Schoolteacher Francis Zaze was part of the Mbati language team that participated in the alpha group of the CAR story-based trauma healing workshop. He noticed that the conflict in Bangui had caused students' behavior to deteriorate. Fights broke out during class and after school. Students openly disrespected their teachers. No amount of discipline seemed to help.

Borrowing from the trauma healing lessons, Francis asked his students to draw pictures of what they had seen. Many drew pictures of guns and grenades. According to Francis, a married father of three,

> *I also did this in the middle school and then let them talk about their fears. Progressively, we noted better behavior, and there was real academic improvement by the end of the year. ... I think these lessons are a very good tool, and I will not stop here. I also want to apply these trauma healing lessons in my own family, with my children and my wife.*

For many survivors like Euphrasie, the suffering lasts long after the initial horror. After she was raped, the man who had wanted to marry her rejected her. Children around her home village taunted her. Euphrasie tried to restart her life in another village, only to be rejected by another potential husband when he heard her story.

Through the workshops, God gave Euphrasie a way to cope with her pain. The workshops are structured around listening and responding to stories and participating in exercises that encourage concepts of forgiveness. Euphrasie said,

> *The young people say often that I have "the disease of the Séléka." I don't know what to do. The only thing that [was] left for me to do [was to] commit suicide. I did not sleep at night, and I always had nightmares. But the lesson of Ama (a woman who experienced the same trauma) and the [forgiveness] exercise ... provide relief. And I have happiness, thanks to God.*

Galen explained that the trauma healing stories in the traditional oral form provide a springboard for Bible translation projects because communities are hearing the material in their heart language. He added,

> *Equipping the church with trauma healing tools is great. We want them to have that. We get involved because it has the potential of being an introductory point where people can see the effectiveness and the relevancy of the Bible in their mother tongue and say, "Now that we have these stories, what can we translate next?"*

* Pseudonym

Footnote:
1. Harriet Hill, Margaret Hill, Richard Baggé, Pat Miersma, *Healing the Wounds of Trauma*, 2013, American Bible Society.

John and Verla York

John and Verla York of Lakewood, Colorado, have been networking people around missions since 1972, when they helped organize funding for a missionary airplane in Brazil. They started the Denver Seed Group (DSG) in 2002 as a way to connect people with the Bible translation movement. Over the next 12 years, the DSG grew to between 30 and 50 people and helped finish funding for 24 translation projects worldwide. The Yorks handed off leadership of the DSG to Bill and Karen Caldwell in 2014, but they remain active in the group. Now in their mid-80s and married almost 65 years, they have four children, 15 grandchildren, and 15 great-grandchildren.

John: We realized Bible translation is built on relationships with other people. And since we had been involved for so many years and made so many friends raising funds for JAARS, people were anxious to join us.

We knew Bernie May through JAARS and had become good friends. When Bernie started Seed Company, we thought it was a great idea. This is where technology and God's timing came together and accelerated Bible translation. We already had a bunch of people who wanted to join us. That's why there was so much excitement in the Denver area. We felt like we were doing what God wanted us to do.

Verla: It was 2002 when we actually got people together and explained how Seed Company works. We would meet in homes. We didn't meet in churches because we wanted it to be a lot of different churches coming together. Our first project was the South Efate language in Vanuatu.

Our worldview has been broadened by the wonderful people we've met as a result of our Seed Company and Wycliffe experiences. So many people don't realize that there are people in the world who don't have any Bible.

John: Bible translation gives you a new perspective of how much the Bible means, when you get involved in supporting this. You read your Bible more. You realize what the Bible really means when people hear it in their own tongue. It makes all the difference in the world.

Happy Hat, by Hyatt Moore

PART IV

REDISCOVERING THE GLOBAL BODY OF CHRIST

CHAPTER 16

INVITING LOCAL COMMUNITIES TO PARTICIPATE

Including broad community feedback on newly translated Scripture yields a more accurate and natural final product. For languages historically disregarded as inferior, the strategy also represents ownership, dignity, legitimacy, and vindication.

When the Jamaican Creole New Testament hit bookshelves in 2012, it was greeted with a collective shrug from many Jamaican churches.

The tepid response made the five Bible translation agencies involved in the project—Seed Company, American Bible Society, SIL, Wycliffe Caribbean, and the Bible Society of the West Indies—ask some serious questions. Namely: why?

They didn't suspect people were ignoring the final product. Jamaica has many churches that should have been snapping up copies like crazy. When they considered how the New Testament was translated, they saw the problem—they were using a traditional approach.

The Jamaican Creole Psalms project invited feedback online from a large group of Jamaican Creole speakers, which greatly increased receptivity to the final product.

Photo: Susan Swafford

In the traditional method, translators work for months at their computers, with only sporadic visits to the outside community (usually with a small group of people) to check the naturalness of their word choices. However, when the translation agencies weighed that approach against the community's response, they knew something needed to change.

Then, the Bible Society of the West Indies began getting requests for a Jamaican translation of Psalms—a book considered important because it's often used by Jamaicans for weddings, funerals, and many other occasions. That's when they asked Seed Company to help them crowdsource community feedback as a way to create interest in the project from the start. With that mindset, the principle players launched the Jamaican Psalms Pilot Project, an effort to translate 20 to 50 Psalms into Jamaican Creole in a way that invited feedback from a large number of people from different walks of life.

To do that, the agencies created a website that solicited feedback from anyone who wanted to log in. Translators also talked with a deep cross section of Jamaican society: pastors, artists, and musicians; men, women and youths; seminary instructors, linguists, and poets.

"And they didn't come with anything pre-drafted. That was the revolutionary part to me," said Seed Company consultant Gilles Gravelle, who helped supervise the project. "They said, 'Here's a chapter we want to draft. Help us process this.'"

While one seminary professor brought deep knowledge of poetry, young people in the group contributed common figures of speech, Jamaican translator Bertram Gayle said. The youths helped balance the translation team in their use of phrases and to explore variations. That prevented translators from imposing their opinions on the Jamaican language.

"The community group provides diversity rather than large numbers of the same kinds of people," Bertram said. "You could see how different people's gifts function." Translators assembled a draft of 50 Psalms in Jamaican Creole and put it on the Jamaican Psalms website. Once people registered, they could look at what translators had come up with and discuss it. "Crowd-sourcing community feedback meant translators were inviting everyday people to do biblical interpretation (hermeneutics) with them and grapple with understanding Scripture." Gilles said.

"A rough draft was produced by the community with the translators," he said. "Do you see the significance of that? We didn't plan that originally."

From there, people began inviting friends who hadn't commented on the original draft of the Psalms to chime in on the website. Translators then brought the drafts around to an even wider group of people, face to face, and got even more input. That cycle made the draft iterative; every time translators posted a new draft, more people logged on and discussed it.

That allowed Gilles and the Jamaican consultant working on the project to simply observe and confirm the team's good work instead of intervene like a consultant normally would.

"In the end, everybody says, 'Yeah, we think this is good,'" Gilles said. "So the community determined together, with the consultants, with the translators, that it was good."

PARTNER PERSPECTIVE

Bill Williams

Bill Williams is the former CEO of the National Christian Foundation. Prior to that, he served as CEO of Generous Giving. In 2006, Bill retired as a Vice President for the BellSouth Corporation, where he worked for 30 years. In 2017, he stepped off the Seed Company Board, on which he had served for nine years.

God's Word has been important in my life, going back to when I was 9 years old. I would say the verse that comes to mind is, "Thy word have I hid in my heart, that I might not sin against thee" (Psalm 119:11, KJV). I don't know anywhere else in Scripture where it says hide anything in your heart, other than God's Word. The idea of having people groups have God's Word in their heart language provides an opportunity for them to hide His Word in their heart.

I was on the board for nine years and was originally exposed to Seed Company about 11 years ago [2006]. In my head and in my heart, I said, "Well, there's no way to argue with that. There's no way to argue with everybody needing God's Word." It just clicked with me.

In my 20s, someone discipled me. I think the word now is "mentored." A lot of that had to do with Scripture memory and quiet time … and that became a part of my life and became something that God called me to through the decades. That, in my life, has been the single strongest factor for my spiritual growth, just in terms of being in God's Word and being encouraged to be in it by others.

CHAPTER 17

EVERY PERSON MATTERS

Every living language needs God's Word. No people group is too small to matter.

The Makoma people had seen the "JESUS" film before, but not in their mother tongue. It hadn't really made sense. But now a team of translators was drafting the film into their language.

Recording of the script was complete, and the team scheduled a trial run to check its quality. Only translators and voice actors were expected to attend—about 20 to 25 people total. They didn't have a proper screen, but planned to project the film onto a guesthouse wall.

But word got out about the viewing. Five hundred people showed up and crammed into tight quarters, eager to watch. This time, they understood. The message of Jesus was no longer foreign; He spoke their language. And when the film ended, half of the viewers responded with decisions to follow Christ.

That was 2016. A few years earlier, this small people group in western Zambia had no Scripture in their language. And they weren't the only ones. Yet a national Bible organization stated, "Our country has no remaining languages that need

*The Mongu Cluster project in western Zambia is translating
heart language Scripture for five languages that once were not
even considered real languages by other people in Zambia.*

Photo: Seed Company

translation." When asked about language groups in the region, they said, "They're too small to count."

In 2008, Seed Company Field Coordinator Stuart Young was just a newbie when he crossed paths with South African missionary James Lucas. They met at the Wycliffe office in Australia. James was taking a crash course in translation principles. He wanted to translate discipleship training materials into the languages of some pastors in western Zambia.

"You may find it's a little more complicated than you think," Stuart told him. "If you need help, here's my card."

Six months later, Stuart got a call.

Soon, he was in Zambia talking with James and his wife about Bible translation needs. Zambia was already a well-developed country, but progress virtually halted at the edge of the Zambezi River. During the wet season, the river stretches over 40 miles wide. Lying west of the river are thousands of villages with dozens of language groups. Churches existed, but not one had mother tongue Scripture.

Stuart and James met with several pastors from western Zambia. Each gave an impassioned plea, explaining why their language needed Bible translation.

"I'm trying to preach, but they don't understand," Stuart remembered one of them saying. "Let my language be the first choice."

Four languages showed the most need. And churches in those areas already knew what they wanted—Luke's Gospel, Acts, and the "JESUS" film.

Still, crucial pieces for starting the project remained missing. Stuart wondered how he could get such a complicated project off the ground.

A couple of months later, he attended Seed Company meetings in Texas. During a coffee break he struck up a conversation with an older man next to him he hadn't met. His name was Wolf Seiler.

"So, what do you do?" Stuart asked.

"I'm a translation consultant," Wolf replied. "I've been working with a translation team in Nigeria on the 'JESUS' film. But we're nearly finished."

Stuart was looking for this kind of person. He told Wolf about the project in Zambia. Surprised, Wolf said his daughter had just moved to Zambia. He'd been looking for a reason to go there, too.

Just like that, the project had a lead consultant.

But none of the languages had a writing system. Stuart needed a linguist. He was back in Australia when he received an unexpected visit from a former teacher who was working on a linguistics degree.

"I still need hands-on, practical experience," she told him. Stuart had just the spot for her. Soon, she and a colleague were off to Zambia. The impossible project was starting to take shape.

At an initial workshop, another language community was added, but members of the group were hesitant. They weren't sure their language was really a language. A majority tribe consistently belittled them with comments like, "That's monkey talk. You're human. Don't talk like a monkey."

But then the linguist analyzed their language and soon they had a writing system and became part of the Mongu Cluster project. The workshop participants went back and told their people, "We no longer need to feel ashamed. Now we know our language has status and dignity."

And so, multiple translators from five language groups began attending regular workshops. Some traveled more than 15 hours to get there. They came by bicycle, ox cart, canoe, bus, and on foot. But despite long distances and difficult terrain, they all kept returning.

"This showed their confidence in the project and belief in the importance of the work," James said.

Before the project began, the translators said they saw much fighting among various denominations. They'd worried about working with people from different church backgrounds and language areas. But soon their fears dissipated.

"We realized there is one Bible, one faith, one everlasting life," one participant told James. "So we also worked together as one."

When the translators returned home, they carried this spirit of cooperation with them.

Early workshops involved telling and writing down stories from the translators' cultures. This helped them analyze the unique sounds of each language, to ensure each alphabet and writing system was accurate.

Soon, workshop participants were translating the first-ever Scripture portion into their languages. Excitement soared as Luke 10:25–37, the Parable of the Good Samaritan, emerged in written form in the Fwe, Kwangwa, Makoma, Mashi, and Shanjo languages. They were no longer too small to count.

Fred Green

Fred Green is Executive Director of The Bolthouse Foundation, which supports numerous Christian ministries and efforts. Those projects include Seed Company's The Least of These project that has helped fund translation for 195 languages worldwide. He spoke about why Bill and Nora Bolthouse have chosen to fund Bible translation so generously through the foundation and his own convictions about reaching the smallest language groups with translated Scripture.

If we are going to plant churches in unreached people groups, then we need those churches to have the plumb line of Scripture in the heart language of the people. If you don't have those churches anchored in Scripture, they can become heretical or ineffective quickly, based on personalities or just lack of understanding. They could still become unhealthy, even with Scripture, but it seems to me that your probability of having healthy churches is much greater if they're anchored in Scripture.

We're very focused on unreached people groups in our overall giving, and this is just part of reaching unreached people groups for us. If people talk about fulfilling the Great Commission, that's what we really see happening. We're strongly motivated by seeing unreached people groups get reached. We're not in the camp where we're trying to make Jesus come back sooner, as if we could! We just want to be faithful to that task and do this work while we have the opportunity and resources to do it.

CHAPTER 18

BUILDING NATIONAL CAPACITY

Helping national agencies train and fund interns like Nafian Saremo in Papua New Guinea increases Bible translation capacity worldwide.

Nafian Saremo received the best advice of his career in 1987. It just took him a few years to realize it.

Nafian was 33 at the time and driven to make a positive impact on his community in Papua New Guinea (PNG). He thought a position in local government would make that possible. But he had just lost in his first election.

That loss, however, positioned him to work with Jee-Young An, a Korean linguist and Wycliffe worker in PNG whom Nafian had offered to help learn the Gwahatike language and culture.

Public office, Jee-Young told Nafian, would not be the way he would generate the change he wanted in his community. True change, Jee-Young continued, can only occur when the Gospel is accepted and lives are transformed.

Nafian Saremo rose up through Seed Company's internship program to become a Bible translation consultant in Papua New Guinea at age 62.

Photo: Seed Company

Nafian ran for office again in 1989. He lost again. He returned to working with Jee-Young, this time as a translator. But Nafian's heart wasn't in the work. Until the words he was translating eventually changed his heart.

"I realized that I was headed in the wrong direction and a peace came into my being," Nafian recalled. "That's when, in 1991, I accepted Jesus as my personal Lord and Savior."

Nafian has been all-in on Bible translation ever since. He worked on the Gwahatike New Testament project through its dedication in 2000. That year, he started a project that he still oversees for the Madi language.

In 2014, Nafian became a Seed Company intern, joining a program that increases national Bible translation agencies' capacity by helping them provide salaries and advanced training for experienced translators. In 2017, at age 62, Nafian achieved full consultant status. Consultants compare translated Scripture with biblical Hebrew or Greek to make sure the translation is clear, natural, accurate, and meaningful. The need for consultants is great in PNG, with more than 800 indigenous languages spread over 600-plus islands.

Nafian has experienced plenty of trials along the way.

When Nafian became a Christian, his beliefs conflicted with those of traditional Gwahatike culture. He took a strong stand against the mixing of Christian belief and those cultural beliefs. He spoke out against following traditional healing methods. Witch doctors wanted him dead.

"They tried all their witchcraft, using the devil's power to try to kill me," he said. "But nothing happened."

Funding for Nafian's Bible translation work was inconsistent, making it difficult to pay for his children's educational fees and, at times, food for the family.

After Nafian and his family moved to a coastal area of PNG so he could start the Madi project, the cultural changes proved difficult. He experienced health problems, including contracting malaria.

But through it all, Nafian remained committed to God and his calling—and to what had first led him to run for public office.

Nafian has mentored the members of his Madi translation team, praying that God's Word would completely change them inwardly, in their families, and then expand throughout the community.

And he rejoices in the impact his team members have made on their community.

People have come to see them as honest, transparent, and trustworthy.

"In the long run, after so many years," he said, "the community has seen that what we have been holding onto—our faith in Jesus Christ has been very genuine." And now, what does Nafian think of what Jee-Young told him three decades earlier?

"What he told me in the past," Nafian said, "I see that it's true. The only change that can come into the community is when a person's heart is changed by the Word of God."

Jill Anschutz

Jill Anschutz is a freelance communications strategist based in Denver, Colorado. Over more than a decade of mass communications and new media work, she has specialized in influencing public opinion and perception. She is a member of Fellowship Denver Church, where she serves as a deacon. She has served on the Seed Company Board of Directors since 2016.

My first job was for a nonprofit that was doing Christian ministry on the ground in India. Through that experience, I became convinced that the best people to do work on the ground are people from the local culture and the local community. So when I left that role, I spent some time searching for a way to support that type of ministry from America. For me, Bible translation is that gateway. It is a way to equip local Christians and local ministers with the most essential tool of all.

It's very possible that the American Church has had some misconceptions about the level of education it takes or the level of resources it takes to do missions. The American Church is rich in both of those things. I think it took a long time of missionaries working on the ground all over the world to realize that, yes, those things are important and they help, but God works amazingly through anyone, even if he or she doesn't have education and lots of resources.

Engaging with Seed Company has absolutely expanded what comes to mind for me when I think about what God is doing in the world. For a while, I lived in sort of a small Christian world. I knew what God was doing in Denver and in my church and in the lives of my friends and my small group, and those things are rich and wonderful. But being involved with Seed Company has taken that and just blown it up. Along with that, I think my faith has grown. … What I'm willing to trust Him for and hope for has expanded along with this much bigger picture of ways that God is working, transforming people, transforming cultures all over the world.

CHAPTER 19

RISING LEADERS

Local and national ownership of Bible translation is fundamental to the work's success and sustainability.

Two convictions animate Dr. Paul Opoku-Mensah: opportunity and urgency.

As director of the Ghana Institute of Linguistics, Literacy and Bible Translation (GILLBT), Paul is mobilizing Ghanaian believers to lead a Bible translation movement in their country and beyond.

Ghana also serves as a 21st-century model for the rest of the world: a translation organization and local churches taking ownership of Bible translation for their own people.

This didn't happen overnight. In 1961, the University of Ghana and SIL International signed a historic agreement to partner in research and language development, laying the groundwork for Bible translation. The next five-plus decades saw completion of 29 New Testaments and the beginning of Old Testament translation. Fourteen of Ghana's 81 languages now have the complete Bible.

Paul Opoku -Mensa, director of the Ghana Institute of Linguistics, Literacy and Bible Translation (GILLBT), speaks at a gathering in Ghana in 2014.

Photo: Seed Company

Paul speaks highly of the expatriate linguists and translators who devoted their careers to bringing God's Word to Ghana's language communities. When Bible translation first began here, the Church was small and its capacity to serve was limited.

Things look dramatically different now. Ghanaians are planning for and staffing the next era of Bible translation. The GILLBT staff alone includes two linguists, two literacy specialists, and 10 certified translation consultants (five expatriates and five Ghanaians), with seven more consultants in training. A scholars program in partnership with Seed Company is equipping Bible scholars and linguists to serve as consultants. In addition to training programs in Africa, GILLBT is also sending trainees to Israel for studies in biblical Hebrew.

"With this pool of personnel and those from other partner organizations, we will have consultants to finish the task," said Kwame Nkrumah, GILLBT's Director of Field Programs. He estimates it will take about 20 more years to translate Scripture for all of Ghana's languages, but there's always the chance that ongoing research will reveal additional translation needs.

In Paul's view, as the Church's numbers and maturity have grown, so too has its responsibility. Ghanaian believers, he said, must take up the mantle of leadership, set the agenda, and lead.

"Fifty years ago, there was hardly a church in Africa," Paul said. "Now we have vibrant churches. When God blesses you, He doesn't bless you to just sit down and celebrate. You must extend that blessing forward."

GILLBT also hopes to change traditional funding patterns. The organization is working to raise awareness among Christian business people. Ghanaian financial partners recently pledged $5 million USD for translation work in Ghana.

This doesn't mean an end to international partnerships—only a shift in roles. Kwame foresees Westerners increasingly responding to invitations to partner with African organizations, as the Macedonian church requested of the Apostle Paul in the Book of Acts. GILLBT's leadership is working toward a future in which their organization supports Bible translation throughout the continent. According to Paul Opoku-Mensah,

Historically, organizations like ours have been transmission belts for missionaries, for ideas, for strategies. But today we are ready to also

participate in the whole Bible translation movement—as agents, not just as transmission belts. We are mobilizing the whole country around the idea that Bible translation is not an American, or Western, task. It is the responsibility of every Christian in every country. As Christians in Ghana, we have a responsibility to ensure that our people get the Bible.

Kwame feels the same way:

It is no more the Western world saying, "We have come. Can you come and help us?" It is this time saying, "Hey, we are on our way. Can you come over and assist us so that we can accomplish the task?" Personally, that's the way I see things happening, and I think my view is also the view of my country and other African countries.

It has taken time for partner organizations to arrive at a shared vision, but Paul sees God at work in changing perspectives. At just the right time, Bible translation organizations were speaking the same language and were prepared to partner with GILLBT in new ways.

"Seed Company has come forth as a natural ally for the kind of vision we had," Paul said.

He is determined to boldly steward the gifts with which GILLBT has been entrusted:

He's given us this unique, historic opportunity. But I am also very conscious that the moment that you don't take [it] He will raise up someone else to do it. So, part of my own energy that drives me is this feeling of being, in a sense, in God's timing. God is helping us and wants us to run with this quickly.

Katherine Barnhart

Katherine Barnhart serves in a variety of organizational roles, but she rarely shares those details in casual conversation. Rather, she is likely to introduce herself as a person with a few important identities. You might hear her say, "You know, I'm a loved child of earthly parents, but also of my loving Heavenly Father. I'm the happy wife of my closest friend, Alan, and grateful mother to our six precious children. I'm a sister and friend of Jesus, along with our spiritual family near and far. And, oh yes, my newest and incredibly wonderful identity is Grandmother!" Both Katherine and Alan live to humbly serve as the Lord leads, with a special joy in kingdom stewardship. This joyful sense of stewardship responsibility is woven throughout Katherine's identity. The Barnharts steward generously and strategically through GROVE Group, an affiliation they developed to invest profits from the company they built with kingdom purposes in mind.

I remember when I first really learned about the ministry of Bible translation during the Billy Graham sponsored Amsterdam 2000 event. I simply hadn't been aware of the need—and the number of Bibleless people groups in the world. If you would have asked me if the job of Bible translation was done, I would have responded, "We're just tying up the loose ends." Then, I learned how much work was ahead, with thousands of Bibleless people groups still on the planet.

Well, I felt the need to repent and join the Lord in this critical, Great Commission task. After all, how can people participate in the Good News—how can they experience real transformation—if they haven't heard it clearly? And how can they hear clearly if it doesn't exist in the language they actually understand at a heart level? I was flabbergasted. This is such a foundational aspect of all fruitful ministry. True transformation is based on Scripture. Everything else follows.

So we were excited to explore partnership with Seed Company as we learned about their focus on Scripture, Bibleless people groups, and equipping local believers. Their values and passion were in alignment with ours. They get us. We share real relationship and priorities. They honor our core values, and we love joining God in accelerating access to Scripture for those still waiting. Seed Company hears our heart and responds to our strategic goals.

Our passion for the Bibleless people of the world and for the Lord Himself has grown as a result. We are friends, colleagues, and true partners in kingdom work. We pray together, serve together, and encourage one another to endure in the race before us. It has been a deep and meaningful journey over the years—transformational for the Bibleless, for us, and for our colleagues in GROVE Group as we serve the Lord together.

CHAPTER 20

EMPOWERING PARTNERS

Global Initiatives puts top priority on equipping and empowering Bible translation partners worldwide.

Luis Chávez Aquino's title hasn't changed, but he brings a fresh outlook to his role as President and Chief Executive Officer of the National Union of Indigenous Translators (UNTI) in Mexico.

"We are not alone any longer," he said.

Luis used to spend all of his time in administration. Today he's able to focus on external relations—primarily financial partners, his board, and organizational government—and he has delegated the day-to-day running of UNTI to a capable leadership team.

Consulting with Seed Company's Global Initiatives team has helped UNTI grow its ministry capacity while slotting people in roles that fit their strengths and calling. UNTI's office more than doubled in size from 2014 to 2017, from six to 15 staff members. In addition, UNTI—a charter partner with Seed Company's Global

Luis Chávez Aquino is the President and CEO of UNTI, the
National Union of Indigenous Translators, in Mexico. UNTI was
one of Seed Company's first Global Initiatives partners.

Photo: Esther Havens

Initiatives team—took on partnerships with 100 new indigenous translators and leaders across Mexico.

The growth coincided with UNTI's involvement with Global Initiatives, which Luis credits with helping him and the organization grow and mature. According to Luis, who has led UNTI since 2009,

> *Global Initiatives is definitely, for us, an answer, a response from God to our need and to our call. With Seed Company and other organizations, God called us to serve and to bring God's Word to every single community, every single language, in Mexico and beyond. But how could we do that? It's a big, big task.*
>
> *When we thought and we were wondering how we were able to grow and to strengthen the organization, how we could grow to accomplish our call, [that] is when Global Initiatives started. And we asked for support from Global Initiatives. Since we started until now, it's definitely been a blessing.*

Many Bible translation agencies outside the U.S. were founded with dependency on outside funding sources. For some, their license to operate virtually mandated that their money come from Western donors, said Mark Farr, Vice President of Global Initiatives for Seed Company. To bolster the viability of Bible translation worldwide, Global Initiatives focuses on helping partners cut that dependence—the very change that many of them have desired for years.

Seed Company's charter Global Initiatives partners were well on their way to doing just that. They just needed the push.

"Typically, where the resources come from is also where the vision comes from—and the marching orders," Mark said. "We realized that it was their desire to engage with the church in their context in a deep and meaningful way, and see Bible translation become the church's own work.

"They had that desire, to have vision that came from their own countries—not to just relay our vision, relay our financial capacity, but to engage the church there."

Part of Global Initiatives' role is consulting leaders of partner organizations on topics such as leadership, fundraising, and general operations. Global Initiatives' whole purpose is to help partners lead Bible translation efforts in their own countries in a way that fosters sustainable transformation.

UNTI has put that goal front and center. Luis stated it this way:

> *To have the opportunity to be involved with more native translators— more native people, too—in Bible translation, and working among their own communities, is great. If we are strengthened as individuals, as leaders, as organizations, in the future we will be more effective. And we will be able to bring God's Word to every community, to every language in our country and beyond. We can be part of a greater thing, of a greater vision.*

With this desire among translation partners becoming more obvious, Seed Company's idea for Global Initiatives began percolating in 2013. That's when then-President Roy Peterson announced an agency-wide Bible study on generosity. The idea spawned deep discussions across Seed Company about how to show generosity to the worldwide Bible translation movement—especially to partners who clearly were ready to take on greater responsibility for translation in their own countries.

"What it makes me think is, God was doing something before we got here," Mark said. "The combination of a global movement of generosity and the church taking responsibility, recognizing Bible translation is central to the mission of the church— those were out there, and we just flowed into it."

Ann McKusick

Ann McKusick is a Founder of Women Doing Well, a ministry of Generous Giving that inspires women to live and give generously. She served on the Seed Company Board from 2001–10 and previously was an executive at World Vision and the National Christian Foundation of California. She credits her involvement with Seed Company for making her aware of the value and the process of Bible translation.

Being on the Seed Company Board was wonderful for my family because the culture is so family oriented. We had board retreats where spouses were included. I've been in ministry many years, and that isn't always the case. The fact that there have been so many opportunities for my husband, Richard, to be a part of the process has meant so much to me. He's been educated and able to grasp the vision, too. So even as we think of our giving—after our lifetime or during—he's always on board with it because he really understands the impact.

I've met the most wonderful people through my partnership with Seed Company. The quality and passion in the field, staff, and executive and board leadership has touched my life. I've been so honored to be among people who are really driven by the Lord's calling to reach His loved ones through Bible translation.

When I think of some of the early leaders, there was such a sense of humility. It was Bible and God first. They placed a high value on people and doing things creatively and God-honoring, trying not to be bureaucratic. In other words, a practical results orientation, but doing it not because we're big achievers, but because we want to be excellent for God—be big achievers for God.

There is an entrepreneurial zest in the Seed Company culture, with an understanding that the results are not just because of how creative we are, but how creative God is in reaching all the people of the world.

CHAPTER 21

GOD ACCOMPLISHES NEW THINGS

From the ashes of a dissolved relationship, new strategies and new local leaders have emerged to reach their people with God's Word.

> *"Time will not wait, and in Nigeria people are eager to have the Scripture in their mother tongue."*
>
> —*Joseph Goje, Director of Language Programs,*
> *Language Development and Bible Translators Association (LDBT),*
> *Bauchi State, northeastern Nigeria*

The National Bible Society of Scotland published the first Nigerian translation of the Bible, Efik, in 1868. For a century and a half, not much changed. Nearly all Bible translation in Nigeria continued to be led by foreigners.

But since the early 2000s, Nigeria's missions landscape has significantly shifted. In July 2017, Danjuma Gambo, translation consultant for Seed Company, shared the progress of Bible translation in Nigeria based on ongoing research collaboration between several organizations. He reported that if translation continued at

*After the dissolution of a key partnership in Nigeria in 2017, more than
a dozen emerging Nigerian translation organizations approached
Seed Company, wanting to take a new role in the work.*

Photo: Darcie Drymon

the current rate, it would take close to 600 years for the remaining 325 Nigerian languages to catch up with present translation projects. This was unacceptable to the Nigerian Church.

A new strategy for translation acceleration was necessary, and that strategy needed to start with the Nigerian people. Instead of relying solely upon Western missionaries, Nigerian Christians determined to drive Bible translation efforts for their country.

For roughly 20 years, Seed Company had worked with translation projects in Nigeria. But when a key partnership in the country was dissolved in early 2017, many wondered about the future of Bible translation in Nigeria.

Yet from the ashes came a surprising development: new Nigerian organizations began approaching Seed Company about partnering in Bible translation projects.

"Every time I went to Nigeria, two or three more organizations would say something to me," said Amy Easterlin, Seed Company's Senior Field Coordinator in Nigeria. "And not just from one little pocket—from different regions, different states. I thought, 'Wow, God's up to something here. He's doing something different.'"

In summer 2017, Seed Company hosted a meeting for emerging translation organizations in Nigeria. Fourteen organizations attended. Joseph's organization, LDBT, was one of them.

"We had been looking for new partners in Nigeria for a year—but nothing. Nothing even coming to the surface. We could shake a tree to kingdom come and nothing fall out of it," Amy said. "And then all of a sudden, they're just miraculously dropping out of the sky."

Forty-one languages exist in Joseph's home state of Bauchi, and many are still waiting for God's Word. Most preaching and teaching is done in either Hausa, the majority language of much of northern Nigeria, or English. But many people who live here don't fully understand either of these languages. Through his work with LDBT and Seed Company, Joseph strives to provide a way for his people to gain a deeper understanding of the Bible through both written and oral translations.

He has already seen the impact that the translated Scripture has on his people. Joseph remembers testing translated Bible passages among language communities in his state. One group was deeply affected by 1 Corinthians 12, which explains how the Church should function as the Body of Christ.

"There were two churches in a particular area that did not get along," he said. "When this passage was read in their language, they resolved to do away with their differences. It became clear to them that the Church is one body with many parts."

Joseph desires to see God transform the lives of all the people of Bauchi through Bible translation.

"In the Church today, we've discovered that people are living lives that are not glorifying the name of God simply because they don't understand the Scripture," he said. "But as they have the Word of God in their language, they will know God better, serve God better, and their lives will be transformed for the glory of God."

Jason Elam

Jason Elam was an NFL kicker for 17 seasons. He won two Super Bowls with the Denver Broncos and was selected for three Pro Bowls. His 63-yard field goal in 1998 tied the NFL record at the time and remains tied for the second-longest in league history. Jason and his wife, Tamy, have four sons and two daughters.

My family was introduced to Bible translation and Seed Company in about 2002 by [then-board member] Todd and Susan Peterson. We quickly became friends with [then-Seed Company President] Roy and Rita Peterson and were infected by their contagious passion for the Bibleless. We learned of a people group that had no Scripture in their heart language and had a population of over 1 million. I was ignorant about Bible translation. The fact that a people group of this size did not have the Scriptures shocked me.

So we partnered with Todd and Susan to begin the Gospel of Luke for these dear people. Not long after this, I had the opportunity to visit the project. My heart became forever rooted in the mission and effort of accelerated Bible translation. What I saw was a group of indigenous believers prepared to give their lives so their people could have the Word of God and so they could have hope and a relationship with the one true God.

It was beautiful, humbling, inspiring, and simply worshipful to observe the heavenly joy these dear ones experienced as they immersed themselves for the first time in hearing God's Gospel that finally had reached their ears, eyes, and hearts.

This is our family's prayer for all the nations—[we have] an urgent desire for all who bear the image of God to readily have the Bible in their native tongue to experience the love their Creator has for each and every one of them.

I am convinced God's desire is for everyone to have His story in their heart language. This indicates much about His character, His nature, and His patience that held fast for centuries before He moved specific saints to risk their lives in the urgent pursuit of Scripture translation. This urgency has only intensified. I believe God has chosen our current generation to eradicate Bible poverty.

CHAPTER 22

CROSSING CONTINENTS LIKE NEVER BEFORE

The Global Church is thinking more globally, and Seed Company is coming alongside. As Christianity's center of gravity shifts southward, believers are expanding their view.

When Bible translators first sought permission to live among the Lahido* people of West Africa, they were met with suspicion. But one respected local leader agreed to give them a chance. He wanted his people to have this Holy Book, and the translators committed to provide it.

The long road to fulfilling that promise has been a journey of trust and discovery for all involved, including a missions-minded church from a country not historically known as a key player in Global Christianity.

The Lahido people have helped shape West Africa's economic and spiritual landscape. Heirs of an ancient tradition, Lahido holy men are viewed as stewards of secret knowledge and power. People travel long distances for their guidance and prayers. Pious families send their sons to study under Lahido religious teachers.

Many people once thought that the Lahido people of western Africa would never have their own translation of the Bible. But thanks to a distinctive partnership with Crossroads Bible Church in Panama City, Panama, a translation team is well on its way to publishing the first heart language Scriptures for the Lahido people in 2019.

Photo: Andres Galvez

Even so, life here is often marred by fear, jealousy, and conflict. In the prevailing belief system, no one can be confident of their standing before God. Most recognize Jesus as a prophet, but only a handful of Lahido people have discovered the hope, peace, and freedom that He offers.

Five thousand miles away, in Panama City, Panama, Crossroads Bible Church has a passion to make that message known. In its first half-century, Crossroads was an English-speaking congregation of expatriates, including many Bible translators. Through those connections, the church played a leading role in Bible translation within Panama.

As the 21st century dawned, the handover of the Panama Canal ushered in a new era for the country. Crossroads, too, was entering a new season. Missions had always been the heartbeat of this church, but now its people purposed to reach farther.

Today, this bilingual congregation of 40 to 50 nationalities and about 25 denominational backgrounds is living out that vision. And they're not alone. As Christianity's center of gravity shifts southward, Latin American believers are mobilizing in increasing numbers to serve among the unreached.

For over a decade Crossroads has focused on making God's Word available to the Lahido people. They partnered with a couple from another local church who were preparing to begin translation. Then, a Crossroads family began to sense that God was calling them to go, as well.

Abraham* and Deborah* had promising careers in engineering and law. Abraham was a church elder. The call wasn't logical, but it was clear.

When Abraham, Deborah, and their three kids boarded a plane for West Africa in 2009, the Crossroads community was sending a family they dearly loved.

"There's a level of excitement and anticipation," said Crossroads missions pastor Ryan Skinner. "We saw God transform their lives. We saw God call them to the mission field. We saw them obey God's calling and to really surrender their careers, their comforts to God's plans."

Others from the congregation have followed, equipped, and sent in partnership with PAAM (Panamanians Reaching the World) to serve in some especially challenging places.

"Their willingness to follow the Lord in this endeavor has had multiple impacts upon us as a church and upon individuals within the church who've seen that," Ryan said. "It's pressed home to them in a way that it wouldn't have been otherwise if some of our really loved people hadn't taken that costly step of going."

The Lahido project has faced serious obstacles. It sometimes seemed impossible that Lahido people would ever have Scripture in their language. But when you talk with Abraham, you can hear the wonder and confidence in his voice. This is God's project, and its success or failure rests in His hands.

Abraham and Deborah originally planned to serve as community development workers. But then the translators and other teammates had to leave the project due to family needs or serious illness. "We were having prayer walks, asking God, 'Okay, what's going to happen now? What is your plan? We want to see your work, and then we can join,'" recalled Abraham.

The door that opened led to an entirely revamped strategy, one which would also require new partnerships. In this critical moment, the Lahido team connected with Seed Company at a conference in Germany. This put them in touch with Seed Company field staff who were excited about the project and the potential for making God's Word available to this influential West African community. Seed Company entered a funding partnership with the Lahido team in late 2015.

With Christians comprising less than 1 percent of the Lahido population, no one expected that finding mother tongue translators would be easy. Moussa*, a professional linguist who had been forced to give up his job due to a disabling illness, agreed to serve as a translator. A God-seeker not unlike Cornelius in the Book of Acts, he comments that the Scripture passages are sweet to his ears.

"You will not find a linguist in every people group you go to," Abraham said. "That's an exception. That was a miracle by itself."

When the team's second translator abruptly left the country, partly due to social pressure, another man, Nuhan*, agreed to take his place.

Moussa favors lofty, traditional language. Nuhan has a more informal style. Bernabe*, the only believer among the three, helps with comprehension checks.

Abraham and Deborah handle accuracy checks and project management.

"It's not a one-man show," Abraham said. "God wanted a team with interdependency."

In 2019, the team plans to publish the first portions of Scripture in the Lahido language—the first installment of fulfilling that long-ago promise. A few young men have responded to the Discovery Bible Study program's French Scripture. But with Scripture in the Lahido language, far more people will be able to participate in a study or engage with God's Word on their own.

Back in Panama, the Crossroads congregation shares Deborah and Abraham's joys and sorrows. They fully expect God's Word to take root and bear fruit among Lahido people.

Ryan explains:

> *I think the people who are most passionate about this and most connected to this work, I think that's one of the things that really excites them. That, for the first time ever, these people are in the process of having access to God's Word. And, from there on, we're really praying and trusting that it's going to spread like wildfire and that through difficulty, through challenges, through suffering even … God's going to be rewriting the history of the Lahido people. And that here on the other side of the world we get to play a role in helping see that happen.*

* Pseudonym

David Daniels

David Daniels has been Lead Pastor at Pantego Bible Church in Fort Worth, Texas, since 2005. During his tenure, he has led the church in supporting Bible translation through Seed Company both in churchwide initiatives and his family's personal giving.

As pastor of a Bible church that, every week, starts with the foundation of God's Word, both for salvation and sanctification, I understand the importance of having the Bible in a person's heart language so that they can hear the Gospel. And God uses the Word. Faith comes by hearing. So it's fundamental for a person coming into a relationship with the living God.

In the 10 years preceding my arrival, our church had unfortunately kind of lost a real sense of mission. So when I came in, over the next four or five years, we began to just gently turn the ship, rediscovering our purpose. [We] began preaching on local and global mission, taking care of the poor, a variety of things that just became layers of what it means for us to be a missional church. In that mix, Bible translation became one of the options for us.

One of the things that stood out for me [during a trip] in Israel was how foundational the Word of God was to God's people—how it was not a tool in their toolkit. It wasn't one of the things that they had in their spiritual life. It was their spiritual life. It was the driver. It was their history. It was their hope. Everything was centered on the Word.

For me, it's just remarkable how foundational the Word was to all of their community and all their life. It helped me to envision that when you move into the New Testament church era, I don't expect that anything really changed for those Jewish believers. The Word, as significant as it was to them as Jews only, now as Jewish Christians, I can expect it was at least that significant for them—if not now even more significant—as they began to connect prophecies and begin to see the fulfillment through Jesus.

Considering Zero, by Hyatt Moore

PART V

RALLYING ALL: THE ACCELERATION OF BIBLE TRANSLATION

CHAPTER 23

STUNNING GENEROSITY

Generosity, humility, interagency collaboration, and a passionate community of givers accelerate the Bible translation movement like never before.

> *"It boils down to whether or not you think what's yours is yours. If you think it's yours, it's really hard to share. If you realize it's not yours and it's God's, it becomes pretty easy."*
>
> *— Dal Anderson, former Chief Operating Officer of Seed Company*

Mart Green found himself arguing against his own cause.

It was late spring 2014, and Green—one of the visionaries behind a forming alliance of Bible translation agencies and resource partners—had been in a mental "dark room," trying to develop a fundraising event connecting more resources and donors to Bible translation.

And now Todd Peterson, Seed Company Interim President and CEO, was on the phone suggesting that Seed Company should give its largest fundraiser—illumiNations—to the Bible translation movement.

Using an illustration that he helped to make famous, longtime Seed Company partner Kwame Nkrumah speaks to an illumiNations gathering about the reality of the blank Bible for millions of people worldwide.

Photo: Seed Company

Mart, Founder of Mardel Christian & Education and Chief Strategy Officer for Hobby Lobby, had been invited by Todd to attend illumiNations 2014 that April. Mart watched in wonderment as Seed Company's partners invested $21 million that weekend. Still, he could only tell Todd of the flaws in his idea.

Todd was an interim president, Mart contended, leading the organization through transition as it searched for a new president. Mart wondered if the Board would approve letting go of the organization's primary funding source. After attending illumiNations, Mart concluded that he did not want to create a separate fundraiser that would compete with what God was clearly doing. Instead, Mart wanted to be a part of God's blessing the nations through illumiNations.

"He's giving me a way out of my dark room," Mart recalled, "and I'm arguing him out of it."

To Mart, Seed Company had discovered how to raise money through a world class gathering of its most passionate financial partners and would be wise to keep doing so. He could understand Seed Company showing other agencies how to do the same, but give illumiNations to the broader Bible translation movement?

"I would never have the audacity to ask Seed Company to give illumiNations to the Bible translation movement," Mart said.

Todd called Mart early that September with the same idea, and shortly thereafter, the Seed Company Board approved handing illumiNations over to the broader Bible translation movement.

"I believed it was an obedience issue," Todd stated matter-of-factly. "I believed God said do it."

Todd had served on Seed Company's Board for nine years, including as Chairman for the previous five years, when he stepped into the Interim President role after President and CEO Roy Peterson (no relation) was recruited to lead American Bible Society. Because of Todd's unique perspective, he now sees the origins of illumiNations in 2010, with Bible translation agency leaders and several financial partners meeting regularly for prayer and discussions (strategic planning, of sorts) oriented on accelerating translation.

"As those meetings were occurring into 2011, 2012, 2013," Todd said, "it was a foundation that I look back on retrospectively and see was laid by God to put us into a position to actually see God birth illumiNations."

The name illumiNations represented a shift for Seed Company that, at the time, might have been temporary. The company had first hosted a gathering in Atlanta, Georgia, called the Invitational, that Todd and his wife, Susan, had envisioned in 2007. That proved to be a template for the launching of President's Forums—weekend gatherings designed to connect donors with opportunities for engaging in Bible translation projects.

In late 2013, Seed Company was nearing its 1,000[th] language engaged and planned to celebrate the milestone at Dove Mountain resort near Tucson, Arizona, a few months later. The celebration would carry the name illumiNations, inspired by Isaiah 60:3: "All nations will come to your light; mighty kings will come to see your radiance" (NLT).

Although pegged to the event, the term "illumiNations" symbolized the Bible translation movement as a whole because, then-Chief Operating Officer Dal Anderson said, Isaiah 60:3 is "less of a prophecy, more of a truth."

"It's not what's going to happen, but what is already happening," he said. "And let's celebrate that the nations are coming to the light."

Todd and Mart had become friends in 2008, and their friendship deepened significantly when Todd invited Mart and his wife, Diana, to join a Seed Company Board retreat in Guatemala in February 2010. That made it easy for Todd to invite Mart and Diana to Dove Mountain to relate their passion for Bible translation that had been birthed 16 years earlier at a Bible dedication in Guatemala.

Also, in 2010, Mart had begun his involvement with the Digital Bible Library, a Scripture platform stewarded by United Bible Societies in service to the overall movement. It would be difficult to find a topic that excited Mart more than Scripture and making it available to Bibleless people.

Mart thought he knew what to expect at Dove Mountain based on other major donor weekends he had attended. But what he witnessed in Arizona surprised him.

Three things, in particular, stood out: funding for Bible translation generated through a world-class event, a spirit of generosity that left attendees feeling "blessed when you left there," and the $21 million raised at Dove Mountain—an unheard of amount for such a gathering. (The total reached $40 million with an additional $19 million committed by a group of investors before that weekend.)

IllumiNations was the event Mart had dreamed of since his Guatemala experience. Except for one thing: it wasn't collaborative funding among the various agencies.

Immediately following illumiNations, Todd and Susan traveled to celebrate their 20th wedding anniversary.

"On that anniversary trip," Todd said, "I felt like the Spirit of God said, 'This is not about Seed Company. It's about Bible translation. It's about the Bibleless people of the world.'"

After the trip, he continued to pray about God's plan for illumiNations. Meanwhile, Dal said, the company's leaders were taking note of a change in missiologic and philanthropic realities. The Global Church had strengthened and was moving into rightful local ownership of Bible translation. Philanthropists were expressing desire to invest in what was locally sustainable instead of in organizations, transactions, or products.

What those local expressions of the Global Church needed was to build the capacity to ultimately own Bible translation work themselves. To address this, Seed Company started a "second line of ministry" to help organizations and churches see this happen. Local sustainability of the work became the ultimate strategy for bringing heart language Scripture to unreached people groups.

At the same time, Bible translation agencies were experiencing a deepening collaboration—exemplified in the Digital Bible Library—and seeking to eliminate duplication of effort.

Still, Seed Company's gift of illumiNations represented what Todd called "stunning generosity" within the Bible translation movement.

Following Seed Company Board's decision to give illumiNations to the overall movement, the partnering agencies hurriedly transformed the illumiNations scheduled for spring 2015 into a six-agency gathering. A total of $36 million was committed for Bible translation. Then, as this newly forming collaboration of agencies and a few passionate givers worked to host the 2016 gathering in South Carolina, Hurricane Matthew showed everyone that, in Todd's words, "God's ways aren't our ways." IllumiNations 2016 had to be canceled, but investors still gave $14 million.

Mart said illumiNations is "still evolving."

"We're still trying to figure out how to share resources and bring more and more givers together," he said.

Expectations remain high, because through years of experience in business, missions, and philanthropy, Bible translation leaders have observed a trend that follows the type of generosity that led to illumiNations.

"The story," Mart said, "always gets better right after somebody does what you can call 'stunning generosity.'"

Scripture points out time and again, as Todd said, "generosity begets generosity." "God is proving Himself faithful and true and bringing every nation to the light," he said. "What a privilege it is as His people to give to the work of eradicating Bible poverty."

Jon and Esther Phelps

Jon and Esther Phelps are the Founders of Storyville Coffee. Jon is also the Founder of Full Sail University in Winter Park, Florida. They have been Seed Company partners since 2011.

Esther: I took my son, Garry, who was 24 and has Down Syndrome, to a Christian concert that was sponsored by Seed Company. Although I thought I was at the concert for Garry, it ended up changing my life. I watched as Seed Company presented the "JESUS" film and the translated Scripture to a large people group in Africa and cried as I witnessed hundreds of people rejoicing as they heard the Gospel story for the first time. The power of Scripture to transform, heal, and save was evident, and I knew that I would support the translation of the Bible for the rest of my life. There are very few investments on this Earth that have an eternal impact like Bible translation.

Jon: There is no argument about the importance of Bible translation. The Bible itself is the living, powerful Word of God. With such a good organization with a good design spreading the translation throughout the world, we don't need to wonder if it is a good idea. Supporting Seed Company is one of the easiest decisions, from a giving perspective, since we are so sure of its purpose and power.

Esther: Each time we attend one of the illumiNations events, I leave so inspired by the stories of the people who actually receive translated Scripture. I can't wait to tell others about the progress and hope they will join us in this great effort.

Jon: The idea of many organizations all circling together and using best practices is inspiring. So often people make the effort and feel good about how hard they are working, but in anything, especially in the business world, results are what counts. So seeing innovation, technology, cooperation, and efficiency by design really matters to me. We are honored to be a small part of a venture so important to the kingdom.

CHAPTER 24

A KEY TO ACCELERATION

Accurate, reliable Bible translation will be accelerated worldwide by training and equipping more consultants to serve in their own regions.

One of Bible translation's major bottlenecks is a shortage of consultants—people who are trained in linguistics, biblical languages, and Scripture interpretation, and who come behind translation teams to verify accuracy. Historically, projects have been held up for months or even years by waits for consultant checks.

In India, Mandie* embodies a key Seed Company strategy: consultants trained to serve in their own countries and regions with the hope of shortening the wait time and getting accurate Scripture to communities faster. She explained,

> *I've always felt that as a translator there is a tendency to trust or believe only in international consultants. I don't know why. I used to feel the same way. Even if we had an Indian consultant, I used to ask, "Why don't we have someone from abroad?" But later, when I started consulting, I found out that some Indians are really good in checking.*

Mandie*, a translation consultant in South Asia, epitomizes Seed Company's strategy to train consultants around the world to serve in their own countries with the goal of getting accurate translations to Bibleless people groups faster.

Photo: Joel M. Jacob

As an Old Testament translator, Mandie once booked a noted Psalms consultant to come and teach a workshop for her team. The wait time was two years. According to Mandie,

> Today, a lot of the Old Testament translations [in India] are complete, but due to the lack of consultants or unavailability of consultants, and having not been checked, the publishing gets delayed. So, having Indians as consultants speeds up the work. If we Indians can do it, we can finish it quickly. The ones who already are consultants, like me, have too much on their plate and can't spend a lot of time. So more Indians would definitely help.

For about 15 years, Mandie served as a Bible translator along with juggling responsibilities as a wife and a mother of two. But in 2011, it was time to take another step of faith: training to become a translation consultant through Seed Company's internship program.

Mandie's husband, Matt*, a Bible translation software developer, pushed her to take a chance. Mandie shared,

> My husband is my biggest encourager. He saw potential in me where I couldn't see the opportunity. And so, when Seed Company offered me this internship, and Matt found out that I could be used more widely, he started encouraging me to go out. And he took a step back.

Mandie came out of college in the early 1990s with a promising future in chemistry or computer science. But her passion turned to ministry. She was excited about sharing the Gospel and became active in evangelism. She also led a Bible study with a friend.

Mandie heard about Bible translation in 1995 from her uncle, who reintroduced her to two Bible translators she had known as a child. They invited her to spend several months in a remote village and to consider Bible translation as a career option.

The experience caused Mandie to reflect on her evangelism experiences and the people who couldn't understand Scripture because it was only available in the national language instead of their heart languages. Mandie added,

I started thinking about so many people not having a Bible in their language. What about them? It really got me thinking. People who don't have God's Word in their language, how will they know that the Gospel I've preached is true? How will they grow spiritually?

That same year, Mandie also took a linguistics course. She realized that her analytical experience as a chemist and computer programmer applied well to this new field. That's when she became convinced God was calling her to Bible translation work.

She and another single woman moved to a remote village in 1996 to translate Scripture into the local language. At first, they stood out because of their clothing and possessions, but they slowly adapted to what was traditionally acceptable. Mandie focused on translation work and attempting to learn the language while she spent time with local women.

In the following years, Mandie continued her education by taking linguistics courses, and during that time, she met her husband.

In 2002, Mandie and her team completed the first draft of 13 New Testament books in the local language, and another team finished the remaining 14. The teams then worked on revisions for over two years. During this process, Mandie saw the need for translation consultants. She also saw the scheduling obstacles of waiting for international consultants.

In 2011, Mandie became a Seed Company intern and began working as a translation consultant. The arrangement reflected the increasingly common Bible translation strategy of East and West coming together to share knowledge and experience.

"Our concept that only Westerners can do consulting should change," she said. "I'm thankful to Seed Company because they are saying to various partner organizations that here is someone who can check your translation for you, in your own country."

She needed training in theology and biblical languages, so she began taking a distance course from Melbourne School of Theology.

"That education really helped me in knowing the Word," she said. "Some of the papers, like interpretation, really influenced my thinking."

Her training required travel, which meant time away from her son and daughter. Matt encouraged and supported her through the many adjustments. She received approval as a consultant in 2013 and completed the theology program in the following years.

As Mandie checked numerous New Testament projects, she grew in her conviction that India needs the Old Testament. And she knew more consultants would be needed to get Old Testament translations into the hands of the Indian people. According to Mandie,

> *Some of the cultural things the community people follow have a lot of similarity with the Old Testament culture. So it was easier for them to relate with the Old Testament and accept it, rather than the New Testament. Many people consider the New Testament as a Western religion. So to me, the New Testament will be accepted more widely by people if an Old Testament is available in their language. It relates to their culture and living. If not the whole of it, at least portions of it—the relevant ones like Genesis and Ruth. These are the books that are really needed in many cultures.*

For instance, one people group she worked with could relate to the "kinsman redeemer" concept found in Ruth, because marrying a childless woman to continue the family line is practiced in their culture. That connection, Mandie added, allowed the people to understand Jesus as their redeemer.

In 2017, Mandie spent six months in Israel at the Jerusalem Center for Bible Translators in order to learn biblical Hebrew as part of her Old Testament consultancy training.

Her experience, and the need she sees in India, convince her that more women need to become involved in Bible translation. This will require encouragement and tangible help from husbands and other family members. Mandie concludes,

> *For many women, I think the struggle is that we take up a lot of roles—wife, mother, daughter-in-law. We end up being torn between all this. If we completely realize where our strength is, and if we have an encourager to move forward, I would say that many women have the potential to come forward. Of course, our attitude of "I, me, myself" should*

also change. We need to be willing to sacrifice. Like I went for this six-month course. It's a big step.

So if we come out of the perspective of "I, me, myself" and break out of our comfort zones, and if someone says "You go, don't worry, I'm there." Once we hear these words, I'm sure many ladies will come out.

* Pseudonym

PARTNER PERSPECTIVE

Dr. Todd Moore

Todd Moore and his wife, Angela, became connected to Seed Company after attending a "JESUS" film briefing and have been active supporters and advocates since then. Todd, a surgeon, scaled back his clinical practice to serve as a Bible translation consultant.

While I was taking a Perspectives class our church hosted, I was personally challenged to consider the unengaged and Bibleless people of the world. Perspectives helped me consider how my own gifts and abilities might be used to meet those needs and to advance God's kingdom.

At the same time I was taking Perspectives, I attended a briefing for the "JESUS" film. I asked about the hurdles in making the film available in other languages. They told me their bottleneck is translating the Gospel of Luke; their partners like Seed Company are doing a bulk of that work. I had no idea what Seed Company was, but Google did. I was shocked to learn that it was in Arlington, Texas, where we live. God aligned a number of things to plunge me into the world of Bible translation.

My family started as financial partners in a special, but sensitive, part of the world. When we went to one of the President's Forums, we became aware of the critical shortage of translation consultants in translation checking. I sheepishly asked myself, "Why couldn't I do that?"

I had to navigate a number of hurdles since I had no Bible translation nor linguistics experience; I don't even have a seminary degree! But Mike Toupin, a pioneer with Seed Company in Ghana, encouraged me. Dr. Larry Jones graciously supported me in exploring the possibility of becoming a translation consultant and guided me along the way. Roman Stefaniw mentored me in the entire translation process. Over the past five years, I have learned the art of consulting by helping check various translations in [South Asia]. What began as a financial partnership transformed into personal investment.

Bringing God and His Word to the Bibleless is a thrill! I have forged eternal friendships with folks from five different groups, who, just six years before, had no Scripture. To serve these families personally, particularly while I am based in the U.S., has been a remarkable privilege.

CHAPTER 25

"PLEASE HURRY": URGENCY AS A TOP PRIORITY

If there's a dominant guiding theme behind accelerating Bible translation, it's urgency. People are dying without God's Word. If the Global Church truly believes this means what the Bible says it means, we must act. God has given our generation the means to eradicate Bible poverty.

As soon as Chase finished talking, the Yef* villagers crowding around him erupted in chatter.

Chase had just explained, with help from his two national traveling companions, why he had come to this remote jungle village. He and his wife, Kelli, wanted to learn the Yef language, teach them to read and write, and translate God's Word into their language.

It was March 2010. Chase and his family had just arrived on this tropical Southeast Asian island the previous December. On this, his first trip to a Yef village, his news had stirred a mini firestorm among the 60-some villagers, virtually none of whom

*The Yef people now have 50 orally translated Bible stories in their heart
language. The introduction of God's Word through those stories has helped
to transform Yef culture from completely animistic to mainly Christian.*

Photo: Mark Elliott

were literate. Finally, a 20-something man named Yudas stood up. His words would set the tone for Chase's ministry, which continues to this day.

"What you're telling us is great news, and they're all excited about it," Chase recalled Yudas saying in the national language. "But please hurry."

Yudas then pointed to several Yef elders sitting around the room.

"Do you see these people?" Yudas said. "They don't speak a word of [the national language]. And they will die soon, having never heard God's words."

That encounter lit a fire under Chase that has guided his work among the Yef people ever since. After moving his family to another Yef village in 2012, Chase helped launch a OneStory Oral Bible Storytelling project with two Yef translators. That project yielded 50 key Bible stories in the Yef language.

Chase and Kelli came to the country with a good idea of what they'd signed up for—the hard work, the time commitment, and all the principles of Bible translation they'd learned during their Wycliffe training. But until that village meeting, it was all theory. According to Chase,

> When Yudas stood up and said that, it became really personal. That's probably the defining moment that really pushed us toward orality. It wasn't an outsider's point of view. It was an insider's view, saying, "We need this. These people right here, they need this. This is their hope." A lot of times, we come with an outsider's view. We think we know what they need. But when they're telling us to hurry, to me, that was really powerful.

Some dismiss oral stories as less-than-legitimate Bible translation. But in fact, when New Testament writers referred to the Word—the Greek term is *logos*—they were talking not about words on a page, but a spoken message. The phrase "Word of God" as used in the New Testament literally means the orally proclaimed message of God.

OneStory was the first step in what Chase hopes will be an oral translation of the entire New Testament for the Yef, starting with the Gospel of Luke and portions of Acts. The village has its own church, and virtually everyone in the village has heard the Gospel in Yef.

Chase's hope is to help Yef people handle more and more of the translation process themselves. In the future, he said, the local church should be making the "what's next" decisions.

"This next phase, my hope is that they get a pool of people who really understand translation principles," Chase said. "My hope is that they'll really get how to translate Scripture from a source text into their language."

* Pseudonym

Todd Peterson

Todd Peterson, Chairman Emeritus and past Interim President and Chief Executive Officer (2014–15) of Seed Company, is a leading champion of the vision for and host of illumiNations. Todd played 13 seasons in the NFL as a place-kicker. He and his wife, Susan, were introduced to the Bible translation movement during his NFL career.

Bible translation upended our lives. The path of least resistance for a wealthy person, a person of influence, is to serve yourself, build your own empire, build your own kingdom. That's just the reality of wealth and is magnified in the culture of pro sports. You're told you're the best thing on Earth once anybody recognizes you have athletic ability.

In 2001, Susan and I became exposed to the work of Bible translation and had our lives transformed by the idea that there were, at the time, about 2 billion people who didn't have a Bible. And hundreds of millions without a single verse of Scripture in their heart language. Romans 10 asks, *How can they be saved? How can they believe if they haven't heard?* They can't hear if the Gospel hasn't been translated into their language and until somebody can communicate the Gospel in the language that means the most to them.

We realized we hadn't been created to serve ourselves, but we're created to serve God, build His kingdom, and take the Gospel to the ends of the Earth. That's reframed the ways we steward money, the ways we steward influence, and the intentionality with which we've discipled our children to understand there are two things that last forever: God's Word and the souls of men. And I see Bible translation as the best intersection of those two things.

If our lives are going to matter, then it's going to be because we've given them to what matters most to God and what lasts forever.

AFTERWORD

Even as I tap out these thoughts, I am working through an inner struggle that has been with me for the last three years: that of the Old Testament. There is unrest in me! Most recently, in my study of Revelation 15:3, the reference to the "Song of Moses" had me scrambling back to the Old Testament. Was John alluding to Exodus 15, or Deuteronomy 32, or Psalm 90?

Clearly, there is an expectancy that the Song of Moses, which was carved into the media form of stone tablets, with the sound deposited into human beings, and passing memory from generation to generation, someday is going to be sung with sound and symbols back to God in Heaven.

In fact, that entire section of Revelation 15:1–4 has nine different allusions covering the Law, the Prophets, and the Writings of the Old Testament. Indeed, scholars have suggested that the Book of Revelation alone alludes to the Old Testament perhaps more than 500 times.

But we tend to translate the New Testament first. There are close to 700 full Bibles, and approximately 1,200 New Testament translations in progress. By deduction, we can see that the Old Testament is underserved in both the Bible translation movement and also in the Global Church.

Often, Hebrews and Revelation are the last books to be translated in a given language; however, they are rich with Old Testament allusions and quotes, similar to that of the Gospel of Matthew. If we didn't have the Old Testament and its context, could we translate the New Testament well with meaningful accuracy? We tend to forget that the only Bible that Jesus, the disciples, and Paul had was the Old Testament. What shall we do?

Even as we continue with New Testament translations, I believe that this is the century for Old Testament translations.

> *Will you participate with God in serving the Global Church and local language communities in Bible translation?*

God gifted called individuals into Seed Company. Bernie May had Marguerite Armerding, Bill Wells, Mike Toupin, and Roger Garland. Similarly, Roy Peterson had Mary Borsh, Dal Anderson, Randall Lemley, Lisa Dammon, and Henry Huang.

In the current expression of Seed Company, and through our history, God has gifted into the organization, and indeed into the entire Bible movement, unsung heroes who have toiled and labored. They will be welcomed with joy into Heaven by those who are believers because they have gained access to Scripture.

Will you give yourself to bring the Word alive as others have done?

During Seed Company's May 2017 board meeting, a presentation was made about the need for sign Deaf languages to receive Scripture. There are more than 350 different sign Deaf languages representing over 70 million people. But there is only one visually completed New Testament: American Sign Language. At the present rate of research, progress, and translation, producing a New Testament for another sign Deaf language will take 50 years; a whole Bible will take 200 years.

The Seed Company Board stewarded this "Bernie May" moment by authorizing a new research lab so that we may assist and partner with sign Deaf ministries through accelerated Bible translation in various sign Deaf languages.

Avodah Labs was created by bringing both artificial intelligence and cognitive neuroscience research into view so that motion-captured sign Deaf languages can be decoded, categorized, and recoded through avatar-like figures to provide meaningful and accurate sign Deaf gestures.

Will you give your time, talent, and treasure for the sign Deaf people globally?

From Bernie May's intense season of prayer came forth an organization that straddled two millennia, a hinge entity between two centuries. This instrument, Seed Company, has a unique purpose: to change the status quo in Bible translation. Gaining acceleration and impact in Bible translation has something to do with experimentation, innovation, strategies, and methodologies. But even more, it has to do with listening to God and understanding where He is leading. God alone is the biggest "end user" of His own Word. He has been working among the various language communities already. He is deeply interested in the translated Word. He wants the Living Word to walk around in the neighborhood.

> *Will you join with us to pray and ensure every language will have the Living Word walking in their neighborhood?*

By board policy, Seed Company is a Vision 2025 organization. The founding board of Seed Company desired to serve the entire Wycliffe family of organizations, and indeed the Bibleless people, by faith and through collaboration to see a Bible translation program started by 2025 for every language that needs a translation.

Throughout this book, we have tasted both impact stories and partner stories. We have witnessed people, languages, tribes, and nations encountering and experiencing God. Might it be that God is intending to write His story in and through you? In this effort, we are calling upon you, the Global Church, to toil together Until There Are None. Imagine that day when there are no remaining languages without Scripture, none! Imagine that day in 2025 when every language group is at least at the starting line of having Scripture access. Imagine Christmas Day, 12.25.2025, when all languages can worship God by telling the arrival of Jesus.

> *How will you join with us so that there are no remaining languages without the Scripture?*

Humbly and respectfully, on behalf of the Bibleless people, partners, and our global colleagues,

Samuel E. Chiang

ACKNOWLEDGMENTS

Prayer is foundational, brings alive the impossible, and sustains to the end. Thank you Mary Borsh, Solomon Lujan, and Marjorie Walton for your ongoing prayers.

A book that brings together multiple perspectives that represent a window into what God is doing through His instrument requires both research and thoughtful writing. Thank you Lauren Bortz, Lincoln Brunner, Emma Chmura, Kim Clement, Becca Coon, Barbara Coots, Kim Farr, Ruth Ferguson, Joel M. Jacob, L.D. Thomas, and Judy Waggoner for your meaningful prose so that an anthology was shaped before us.

To the long list of Seed Company staff, partners, and professional photographers who have shot images over the years, thank you for your beautiful and significant work. Melanie Stephens and Michael Currier, your choice of photography provided meaning so that the interplay between words and image provided a heightened sense of supernatural outworking of the Spirit of God.

Thank you proofreaders, web designers, Jim Akovenko, Jessie Davenport, Shane Dennehey, Karen Farney, Adia Harris, Jennifer Hutton, Matt Knisely, Doug Kogler, Becca Lewis, Hope McKeever, Ana Mims, Davis Powell, Shawn Ring, Karen Sandifer, and Shane Shelton for your patience with each iteration of the manuscript. You made things more accurate and purposeful.

Special thank you to Jim Killam and Laurie Nichols! Your superb editing, careful attention to details, and unique perspectives assist the reader to gain a window into Seed Company, and in turn, a window into the heart of God.

To God be the glory!

APPENDIX I
SEED COMPANY BOARD OF DIRECTORS

Past
(in chronological order of service)

Peter Ochs*
John Watters
Steve Shelton
Roy Peterson
Jim Fetterolf
Rick Alvord
Judy Sweeney*
Matt Lees
Ann McKusick
Mark Matlock
Jeff Brown
Todd Peterson*
Michael Stoltzfus
Bill Williams
Lisa Cummins
Freddy Boswell
Samuel Chiang

Current

Joyce Williams**
Rick Britton*
Jeff Johns
Jason Baker
Matt Mancinelli
Robby Moser
Andrea Levin Kim
Jill Anschutz
Kent Bresee
Bob Creson
Michel Kenmogne

* Past Board Chair
** Current Board Chair

APPENDIX II
SEED COMPANY TIMELINE

1991   Wycliffe Bible Translators International recognizes that the traditional model of sending Western missionaries overseas to lead the ministry will not complete the Bible translation task. A focus on national translators and Bible translation organizations gathers momentum.

1992   Hyatt Moore, President of Wycliffe Bible Translators, asks outgoing Wycliffe Bible Translators President Bernie May to become Vice President of New Initiatives.

1993   Partners With Nationals, which soon would be known as Seed Company, begins under Bernie May's leadership as a team within Wycliffe USA. The organization begins with 10 projects funded by 10 financial partners.

1998   Seed Company incorporates.

1999   Seed Company and The JESUS Film Project form the Luke Partnership with 30 initial projects. Seed Company becomes a field-engaged organization. Seed Company Board adopts core values that guide the organization to this day.

2001   Seed Company commits to Vision 2025, an initiative to see a Bible translation program started by 2025 in all languages needing one.

2002   Bernie May retires. James Stamoolis becomes CEO. Seed Company Board votes to move the organization headquarters from Southern California to Arlington, Texas.

2003   Roy Peterson is appointed as President and CEO. Seed Company sets a goal of engaging in 1,000 languages in the coming decade.

2004   A vision plan is approved to engage a total of 1,000 languages in the next 10 years.

2009   Three separate partner categories are identified: Impact, Technical, and Resource partners. The first satellite communications station is established for remote partners.

2014   Seed Company engages its 1,000th language, fulfilling the vision of former President and CEO Roy Peterson and his leadership team. By then, Roy had become President and CEO at American Bible Society. Seed Company Board affirms giving the organization's primary funding event, illumiNations, to the entire Bible translation movement.

2014–15   Todd Peterson serves as Interim President and CEO.

2015   Samuel E. Chiang becomes Seed Company President and CEO, and comes in with focus on the 1,778 remaining languages needing Bible translation to begin. Seed Company's guiding principles for Bible translation are renamed Common Framework and recognized as a key to achieving Vision 2025. Wycliffe USA asks Seed Company to help convert up to 80 percent of its translation projects to this model.

2017   Seed Company Board votes to organize Avodah Labs, a charitable religious nonprofit entity, to accelerate know-how and progress for more than 350 sign Deaf languages representing over 70 million people.

2018   Seed Company engages in its 1,500th language.

APPENDIX III
A COMMON FRAMEWORK FOR BIBLE TRANSLATION:
EXECUTIVE SUMMARY AND FUNDAMENTAL PRINCIPLES

Bible translation is central to the Gospel because the incarnation of Christ is itself an act of translation. It is an integral part of God's mission in this world to reconcile and restore all creation to Himself—to make all things right.

Increasingly, the Church recognizes that God's heart for humanity and for His Church is expressed in every nation, tribe, people—and every language. In this missiological context, Bible translation is not primarily about completing translations.

It's about an incarnate Church working for transformation of the individual, the Church, and community.

Fundamental principles of this framework are:

- Ownership (John 1:14). The local, incarnational expression of the Church owns the vision and responsibility for Bible translation work.

- Partnership (1 Corinthians 12). Translation goals and products are collaboratively determined with partner organizations and the end users.

- Stewardship (Matthew 25:14–30; Luke 16:1–13). Projects are well developed, well resourced, well managed, and accountable.

- Relationship (Philippians 1). Collaboration happens among the people translating God's Word, the people receiving it, and the people funding and praying for the work.

It all leads to:

Accelerated Impact (2 Timothy 3:14–16; John 9:4). A community's needs dictate which passages of Scripture will be translated first—impacting the largest number of people in the shortest possible time, while never sacrificing quality.

Within this common framework, acceleration is not just about reducing the time required to translate a Bible. It is about giving communities faster access to usable Scripture. Short-phased projects—accelerated impact—contribute to an overall plan to fulfill the Scripture translation needs in a people group.

The local church hosts the efforts of other partners: prayer, technical, and financial. All resources—time, talent, and treasure—belong to God. All of us as stewards are equal partners before God for the effective use of those resources, so others can experience the life-changing message of the Bible.

Bible translation is community work: the community of people who speak the language, the community of the believers in that language, and the community of the wider Church participating in God's mission.